SHERLOCK HOLMES

·A CENTENARY CELEBRATION·

SHERLOCK HOLMES

A CENTENARY CELEBRATION

Allen Eyles

1817

HARPER & ROW, PUBLISHERS, New York

Cambridge, Philadelphia, San Francisco, London
Mexico City, São Paulo, Singapore, Sydney

Grateful acknowledgment is made to Dame Jean Conan Doyle
for permission to quote from copyrighted works by the late
Sir Arthur Conan Doyle.

Library of Congress Cataloging-in-Publication Data
Eyles, Allen.
   Sherlock Holmes : a centenary celebration.

   Includes bibliographies and index.
   1. Doyle, Arthur Conan, Sir, 1859–1930—Characters—
Sherlock Holmes   2. Holmes, Sherlock (Fictitious
character)   3. Detective and mystery stories, English—
History and criticism.   4. Sherlock Holmes films.
I.   Title.
PR4624.E9   1986   823′.8   86–45094

ISBN 0-06-015620-1

Published simultaneously in Canada by
Fitzhenry & Whiteside Limited, Toronto

First U.S. edition

Produced by the Justin Knowles Publishing Group
9 Colleton Crescent, Exeter, Devon, U.K.

Designer: Ron Pickless

Contents

INTRODUCTION

One hundred years ago a young Scottish doctor who was in practice at Southsea near Portsmouth in England amused himself while waiting for patients by writing stories. It was thus that Arthur Conan Doyle conceived Sherlock Holmes – the unique private detective who came to assume a reality unequalled by any other fictional character in the world. His literary birth was slow – it was eighteen months before he appeared in print in a novel, *A Study in Scarlet*, and further stories about him did not follow immediately.

But when in 1891 the first of six Sherlock Holmes adventures was published in *The Strand Magazine*, it created an appetite in readers that seemed insatiable and the Baker Street detective so impressed them with the originality of his methods of deduction that every new adventure added to his stature until he had a life of his own, out-grew his creator, resisted all attempts to do away with him and became the larger than life, near-mythic figure of today.

At the time they were written, the early stories of Sherlock Holmes were quite innovative. The tradition of detective fiction was mainly undeveloped and many of Holmes's cases had (or seemed to have) intriguing references to contemporary scandals, and this, coupled with the special characterization of Sherlock Holmes, captured the readers' interest.

Nowadays the stories are not prized so much for their connection with particular scandals as for the inimitable Sherlock Holmes: while the tales have the background charm of evoking the more leisurely Victorian era – fog-bound streets, gas lamps, hansom cabs, of telegrams rather than telephones, of a more unsophisticated Britain with its quaint domestic crimes and lingering family feuds, it is the individuals who live most vividly. Clients, police inspectors, villains, beleaguered ladies and the supporting characters who are such an engaging part of the Holmesian saga, all emerge as believable people. But far more memorable than any of them is Holmes himself. In only one case, *The Hound of the Baskervilles*, is the story powerful enough to be remembered for its own sake.

Sherlock Holmes stands head and shoulders above other detectives. So many rivals – from G.K. Chesterton's Father Brown and Agatha Christie's Miss Marple to Earl Derr Biggers's Charlie Chan and Rex Stout's Nero Wolfe – seem by contrast superficially conceived, relying primarily on offbeat characteristics of vocation, age, sex, size or nationality to make them memorable. In many of their cases, the plots demand most attention and the sleuth becomes less important. Holmes's most notable competitors were the seedy private eyes of the best American detective fiction, especially Raymond Chandler's Philip Marlowe who dominates his stories as Holmes did (who can understand the plot of *The Big Sleep*?).

Undoubtedly, detectives have to escape the confines of print to achieve immortality. Film and television adaptations put them into much wider circulation than type and give them a sense of reality stronger than the visualizations of readers. It doesn't matter that different actors play Sherlock Holmes and Philip Marlowe: in fact, it is a great advantage to the endurance of the characters. Humphrey Bogart may be a better Philip Marlowe than Dick Powell or Robert Mitchum but the conflicting interpretations all suggest that there is no precise, definitive Marlowe. Similarly, because so many actors have played Sherlock Holmes, he belongs to no single performer and there is no *one* Sherlock Holmes – he is bigger than any

The silhouette forms the key to the decorative tribute given to Sherlock Holmes by London Regional Transport at Baker Street Underground Station in passageways and on the Bakerloo Line platforms. The large profile consists of many hundreds of the same profile in miniature.

particular interpretation. The diverse representations turn the character into a myth, all the more real in the mass imagination for not being exactly delineated. And the very fact that Sherlock Holmes has lasted a hundred years works in his favour, predisposing new generations to take him up. His name is helpfully distinctive and unusual – but easily remembered.

There are particular qualities in Sherlock Holmes that make him so attractive beyond his individual quirks and eccentricities. There is his unswerving integrity. He is completely to be trusted. He is sensible and just, not impressed by rank or wealth, and not concerned with financial gain but working for a deeper satisfaction. He is more sensible than the law, more versatile in his methods, more understanding in his judgements than the bench. Beyond all this, he is the apotheosis of the rational, thinking man. He is clear-thinking, decisive, above the pull of emotions, and his intellect astounds us. (Put Holmes in a modern context and his deductions appear absurd but they seem feasible in Victorian times when life was – or so we believe – simpler and more regimented so that – for example – a man's station and profession could be reliably read from his appearance.)

Sherlock Holmes's enduring place in the public consciousness has been immeasurably aided by his distinctive trappings – even in silhouette, the image of a man smoking a curved pipe in a deerstalker hat is recognized the world over. But equally important is the role of Holmes's companion and biographer, Doctor John H. Watson. In his case, the popular impression of him as a blustery nincompoop (based on the way he was portrayed by Nigel Bruce in the fourteen films that starred Basil Rathbone as Holmes) is a false one. But in the performing arts Watson's role is necessarily diminished: Sherlock Holmes is seen directly, he is not presented to us as viewed by Watson. Yet, in the original stories, Watson is essential. He tells us how to respond to the cold, intellectual calculating machine that is Sherlock Holmes, he points out the weaknesses in Holmes's armour – his indulgence in cocaine as a stimulant to relieve tedium, his vanity, his withering contempt for fools – and he makes us like and admire Sherlock Holmes. The truth is that, without the sympathy and understanding extended by Watson, Holmes could become a pretty unpleasant character.

The great detective does not really need Watson, as we see from the long periods when Holmes neglects to keep in touch, letting his old friend think erroneously that he has perished at the Reichenbach Falls and losing touch for years during his early retirement. But, in another mood, Holmes secretly buys up Watson's medical practice through an intermediary so that Watson will rejoin him at Baker Street. Holmes calls Watson his friend – "Except yourself, I have none" – but he never calls him by his first name (and the ever-deferential Watson never dares call him "Sherlock"). As we read the stories, we slowly appreciate Watson's role – he acts as a witness when Holmes draws statements and confessions, and he is often called upon to pack a gun and accompany Holmes on his more dangerous missions. Watson is also useful as a sounding board; regarding the facts of one case, Holmes tells the good doctor, "I shall enumerate them to you, for nothing clears up a case so much as stating it to another person". He finds Watson stimulating, in a round-about way: "It may be that you are not yourself luminous," he tells Watson, "But you are a conductor of light. Some people without possessing genius have a remarkable power of stimulating it." And: "When I said that you stimulated me I meant, to be frank, that in noting your fallacies I was occasionally guided towards the truth."

Watson sums up his "humble role" in the partnership after receiving a summons to Baker Street which reads "Come at once if convenient – if inconvenient come all the same. – S.H." Watson writes:

He was a man of habits, narrow and concentrated habits, and I had become one of them. As an institution I was like the violin, the shag tobacco, the old black pipe, the index books, and others perhaps less excusable. When it was a case of

The celebrated silhouette, posed here by Basil Rathbone.

active work and a comrade was needed upon whose nerve he could place some reliance, my role was obvious. But apart from this I had uses. I was a whetstone for his mind. I stimulated him. He liked to think aloud in my presence. His remarks could hardly be said to be made to me – many of them would have been as appropriately addressed to his bedstead – but none the less, having formed the habit, it had become in some way helpful that I should register and interject. If I irritated him by a certain methodical slowness in my mentality, that irritation served only to make his own flame-like intuitions and impressions flash up the more vividly and swiftly.

Perhaps the real secret of Holmes's tolerance of Watson lies in Watson's awestruck appreciation of his skills ("My dear Holmes!" he so often exclaims in amazement), and in his role as biographer: "I am lost without my Boswell," says Holmes, and "I will do nothing serious without my trusted comrade and biographer at my elbow." Although he declares, "I like to work anonymously and... it is the problem itself which attracts me," and although he allows the police to take all the credit for solving cases, it is Watson, in publishing accounts of his work (even though they are, according to Holmes, too romantic and sensationalized), who provides him with the long-term recognition that he secretly desires. (In addition, Watson suggests that "so long as he was in actual professional practice, the records of his successes were of some practical value to him".) We know from Watson that Holmes is "as sensitive to flattery on the score of his art as any girl could be of her beauty"; we see how he summons Watson, after many years without contact, to witness the triumphant conclusion of his last case.

As for Watson, he has a lot to contend with, such as Holmes's silent moods and his untidiness (he skewers his unanswered letters to the mantlepiece, keeps his cigars in the coal-scuttle, and puts criminal relics in the butterdish). The doctor remonstrates with Holmes only over his habit of peppering the wall with bullets, remarking to us, his readers, "I have always held that pistol-practice should be distinctly an open-air pastime." Only when Watson faints with shock at the sight of Holmes alive after all, three years after his apparent end at the Reichenbach Falls, or

Sherlock Homes as he was seen by two of the best known of the illustrators of the original stories – Sidney Paget (below) and Frederic Dorr Steele (centre below).

when the Doctor is wounded on a case, does Holmes express concern, though there is warmth to their reunion on his last case: "Good old Watson! You are the one fixed point in a changing age."

Watson claims a "natural Bohemianism of disposition" and delights in the opportunities to participate in Sherlock Holmes's cases. Even when married to a former client, he finds opportunities to join up with Holmes, and his medical practice never seems to prove an obstacle: Watson has a fellow doctor who is "an accommodating neighbour". But we are certainly given cause to wonder how devoted a physician Watson is when he leaves injured and shocked figures in two of the stories in order to follow Holmes and see the chase through to the end. If Watson receives little satisfaction from his medical career, it is easily inferred that he benefits considerably from his association with Holmes. It is Watson's sole claim to fame. Like the engineer in one of the cases who can entertain people for the rest of his life with the story of how he lost his thumb, we can imagine Watson basking in the renown that comes from being the celebrated detective's biographer as well as enjoying the financial rewards from publishing the accounts, so popular that Holmes is a national celebrity. "I hear of Sherlock everywhere since you became his chronicler," says the detective's brother Mycroft.

That Sherlock Holmes has remained so popular, some sixty years after the last story appeared, is a tribute to the sheer readability of the stories, and the inspiration that they have given film-makers, novelists and playwrights to produce adaptations, parodies and pastiches. On top of this, there is the ever-increasing volume of scholarship about Holmes. There have been slack periods when the original stories have continued to sell without the impetus of new developments, but they have been rare.

This book surveys the highlights of the first hundred years of the Sherlock Holmes phenomenon. It examines the creation of Holmes and the evolution of the canon of sixty tales – four novels and fifty-six short stories – and it seeks to demonstrate the ways in which, with varying fidelity, the basic concept has been used since and how the popular impression of Holmes has been changed.

Sherlock Holmes as he has been portrayed by various actors – (left to right) William Gillette, Eille Norwood, Basil Rathbone and Jeremy Brett.

1 THE FIRST STORY
A STUDY IN SCARLET

When the first Sherlock Holmes story, *A Study in Scarlet*, was written at Southsea, on the south coast of England, in 1886, Arthur Conan Doyle was 26 years old, having been born in Edinburgh on 22 May 1859. He had arrived at this mainly residential part of Portsmouth four years earlier, having chosen to set up in general practice on his own as a doctor here (he had previously assisted in a practice at Plymouth). He found suitable vacant premises in an eight-roomed house called 1 Bush Villas. This was one of a row of identical properties at the end of Elm Grove, a tree-lined main thoroughfare, and Conan Doyle paid a rent of £40 a year to the Baptist church next door. He put up a brass plate and a red lamp, and opened for business in June 1882. He had considerable spare time as patients were less than plentiful, and some of it he used to write short stories.

Creative endeavour was in the blood. His grandfather, John Doyle, had been a famous caricaturist, and three of his uncles had made artistic careers. One of them, Richard, was a well-known illustrator for books and for *Punch* magazine. Arthur's father, Charles, the family failure who had retreated to Edinburgh and turned to alcoholism, had been a designer, architect and book illustrator. Arthur's stories were good enough to be published in magazines, although most appeared without name credit, and he did not earn enough to consider writing as more than a sideline. He became a member of the Portsmouth Literary and Scientific Society in the winter of 1883 and had joined its Council by 1885, later becoming joint Honorary Secretary. The ground floor at 1 Bush Villas was occupied by a housekeeper, and other rooms were occasionally used by resident patients. On 6 August 1885, Conan Doyle married Louise Hawkins, the sister of one of these patients.

With the added responsibility of a wife, Conan Doyle decided to make a greater

The house (right) where the literary birth of Sherlock Holmes took place: 1 Bush Villas, Elm Grove, Southsea. Arthur Conan Doyle may be seen standing at the front gate, with others in residence gathered at the windows. The drawing of Conan Doyle sweeping the path (far right) accompanied the publication of his memoirs in *The Strand Magazine*, and appeared in the November 1923 issue. The plaque on the railings to the right of the entrance reads "Dr Conan Doyle: Physician & Surgeon". In later years, the ground floor (except for the entrance) was extended forward to become a shop with a separate front door. The entire row of houses, together with the adjacent church, was destroyed by the Blitz in January 1941. A modern block of flats now occupies the site (opposite the end of Green Road) and in 1983 a plaque (above) was placed on the brickwork.

effort to develop a literary career, for his income as a doctor was barely sufficient to maintain a household. He knew that he had to make a name for himself by publishing a longer work. He was an admirer of the detectives created by Edgar Allan Poe (Auguste Dupin) and Emile Gaboriau (Monsieur Lecoq), as well as of the work of Wilkie Collins (*The Moonstone*, *The Woman in White*) and Israel Zangwill. But he wanted to do something different, and his inspiration for this was Doctor Joseph Bell, the surgeon and teacher of medicine during his student days at Edinburgh University. "Reading some detective stories, I was struck by the fact that in nearly every case their result was achieved by chance. I thought I would try my hand at writing a story where the hero would treat crime as Doctor Bell treated disease, and where science had taken the place of chance. The result was Sherlock Holmes . . ."

Conan Doyle described Bell's methods:

He would sit in the patients' waiting room, with a face like a Red Indian, and diagnose the people as they came in, before even they opened their mouths. He would tell them their symptoms, and would even give them details of their past life, and he would hardly ever make a mistake.

An example of Bell at work in front of his students:

"Ah," Bell would say to one of his patients, "you are a soldier, and a non-commissioned officer at that. You have served in Bermuda. Now how do I know that, gentlemen? Because he came into the room without even taking his hat off, as he would go into an orderly room. He was a soldier. A slight authoritative air, combined with his age, shows that he was a non-commissioned officer. A rash on his forehead tells me he was in Bermuda and subject to a certain rash known only there."

Sherlock Holmes was given the same powers of observation, which he demonstrated to numerous clients and to Dr Watson at their very first meeting. Of great practical benefit to Conan Doyle was the intimate knowledge of crime, criminals and corpses that he had gained from another lecturer in Edinburgh, Sir Henry Little-John, who taught forensic medicine and was the City's Police Surgeon.

The name Sherlock Holmes took time to evolve. Conan Doyle did not know what to call his detective at first. "One rebelled against the elementary art which gives some inkling of character in the name, and creates Mr Sharps or Mr Ferrets. First it was Sherringford Holmes; then it was Sherlock Holmes," he said in his reminiscences. The name Holmes was very likely suggested by the American jurist and medical pioneer, Oliver Wendell Holmes, whose impending visit to Europe was in the news – his authorship of monographs, his expert knowledge of tobacco and his analytical mind were all features that Sherlock Holmes shared.

As a cricket enthusiast and player, Conan Doyle would have known of the Nottinghamshire players Sherwin and Shacklock, who may have jointly suggested the detective's first name, and there was also a Devon cricketer actually called Sherlock. But it seems as likely that the name came from a prominent violinist, Alfred Sherlock, as Conan Doyle's sleuth also played the instrument.

Mindful of Lecoq's dim-witted associate, Father Absinthe, and also perhaps of Don Quixote's companion, Sancho Panza, Conan Doyle went on: "Holmes could not tell his own exploits, so he must have a commonplace comrade as foil – an educated man of action who could both join in the exploits and narrate them. A drab, quiet name for this unostentatious man. Watson would do. And so I had my puppets and wrote my *Study in Scarlet*." It is worth noting that a member of the Portsmouth Literary and Scientific Society was a Doctor James Watson, who had practised in Manchuria before retiring to Southsea, and who was certainly known to Conan Doyle. The name Watson did not register immediately; in early notes for the story, he was called Ormond Sacker.

Dr Joseph Bell, who was the primary inspiration for Sherlock Holmes.

A Study in Scarlet

Ormond Sacker - from Soudan. from Afghanistan
Lived at 221 B Upper Baker Street
with
I Sherrinford Holmes -
The Laws of Evidence
Reserved -
Sleepy eyed young man - philosopher - Collector of rare Violins
An Amati - Chemical laboratory
I have four hundred a year -
I am a Consulting detective -
What rot this is" I cried - throwing the volume
: petulantly aside " I must say that I have no
patience with people who build up fine theories in their
own armchairs which can never be reduced to
practice -
Lecoq was a bungler -
Dupin was better. Dupin was decidedly smart -
His trick of following a train of thought was more
sensational than clever but still he had analytical genius.

Arthur Conan Doyle at his desk, allegedly writing *A Study in Scarlet* in 1886. Above right is a page of Conan Doyle's notes for *A Study in Scarlet* – he has yet to settle on his final choice of names for Sherlock Holmes and Doctor Watson. Note the dismissive reference to earlier sleuths LeCoq and Dupin, which were voiced by Sherlock Holmes in the story.

It was on 8 March 1886 that Conan Doyle began outlining the story, which he initially called *A Tangled Skein*. He worked away in the tiny study at the top of the house and did the real writing in three weeks, adopting what became his customary method of working backwards from the solution. He worked at all kinds of hours – between patients, early in the morning, late at night – but made few alterations to the handwritten sheets, finishing the story before the end of April. It was an awkward length – too long for a magazine, too short to encourage publication on its own – and there was difficulty in getting it accepted.

Finally, an offer came from Ward, Lock & Company, dated 30 October 1886: "We have read your story and are pleased with it. We could not publish it this year as the market is flooded at present with cheap fiction, but if you do not object to its being held over till next year, we will give you £25 for the copyright." Even more discouraging than the paltry amount and the absence of a royalty was the delay in publication. However, Conan Doyle reluctantly signed away all rights in *A Study in Scarlet* on 20 November 1886 for £25 and never received a further penny for it. A full year ensued before it was published as the principal attraction in *Beeton's Christmas Annual*, which sold out in a couple of weeks. The story was illustrated by D. H. Friston, who thereby became the first artist to depict Sherlock Holmes. In July 1888, Ward, Lock & Company reissued the story on its own as a genuine "shilling shocker", a paperback priced at one shilling. Charles Doyle, working from inside the asylum where he was confined for his alcoholism, provided six line drawings that, regrettably, were awful. For the first and last time, Sherlock Holmes was depicted with a beard!

A Study in Scarlet gives us a very thorough introduction to Sherlock Holmes and Doctor Watson. It is presented as "Being a reprint from the Reminiscences of John H. Watson, M.D., Late of the Army Medical Department", and it begins with Watson providing a short autobiographical sketch, describing how he is on leave to recover from the effects of injury and illness while serving during the second Afghan war. Lacking friends or relatives, Watson can no longer afford to stay in a London hotel, and a former acquaintance, whom he meets in the Criterion Bar at Piccadilly Circus, knows of someone wanting to share lodgings. Someone who is, however, "a little queer in his ideas" and full of "a lot of out-of-the-way knowledge", and who, moreover, conducts strange experiments, like beating corpses to discover how far bruises may be caused after death. We can hardly wait to meet such an intriguing figure, and it is in the chemical laboratory of a London hospital that one of the most significant and memorable introductions of all literary history takes place.

"Dr. Watson, Mr. Sherlock Holmes," said Stamford, introducing us.

"How are you?" he said cordially, gripping my hand with a strength for which I should hardly have given him credit. "You have been in Afghanistan, I perceive."

"How on earth did you know that?" I asked in astonishment.

"Never mind," said he, chuckling to himself.

When *A Study in Scarlet* was published on its own in England for the second time in 1891, it was extensively illustrated by George Hutchinson. He depicted Holmes coming forward to shake Watson's hand on their very first meeting. A plaque (above) at St Bartholomew's Hospital – Bart's – in London commemorates the occasion. Provided in 1953 by American enthusiasts, it is on an office wall where it is not immediately accessible, but it may often be viewed upon request, and it is lit up with its own spotlight on special occasions.

They agree to share the rooms that Holmes has found at 221B Baker Street, but it is some time before Watson discovers his companion's profession. After ridiculing a magazine article about the powers of observation and deduction, he learns that Holmes was its author. ". . . I have a trade of my own," says Holmes. "I suppose I am the only one in the world. I'm a consulting detective." And he explains how he knew that Watson came from Afghanistan:

> The train of reasoning ran, "Here is a gentleman of a medical type, but with the air of a military man. Clearly an army doctor, then. He has just come from the tropics, for his face is dark, and that is not the natural tint of his skin, for his wrists are fair. He has undergone hardship and sickness, as his haggard face says clearly. His left arm has been injured. He holds it in a stiff and unnatural manner. Where in the tropics could an English doctor have seen such hardship and got his arm wounded? Clearly in Afghanistan."

This illustration for *A Study in Scarlet* (right) accompanied its first publication in *Beeton's Christmas Annual*. D. H. Friston shows an unfamiliar Holmes with long sideburns examining the mysterious message written in blood on the wall of the room where the corpse of Enoch J. Drebber has been found. Inspector Lestrade is gesturing towards the wall, while the others are Doctor Watson and Inspector Gregson. The same scene as depicted by George Hutchinson in 1891 (far right) shows Lestrade holding a lighted match for Holmes and Watson to observe his find.

Holmes informs Watson that the police inspectors Lestrade and Gregson are apt to consult him over difficult cases: the two men are "the pick of a bad lot. They are both quick and energetic, but conventional – shockingly so." In fact, it is Tobias Gregson who invites Holmes to Brixton to see the body of an American, Enoch J. Drebber, which has been found in an empty house. From this first story we find Holmes venting his sarcasm on the police. Disgusted at the way the path to the house has been trodden over by the force, he remarks with acid humour to Gregson, "With two such men as yourself and Lestrade upon the ground, there will not be much for a third party to find out." Later he interviews the policeman who found the body and cruelly informs him, "I am afraid, Rance, that you will never rise in the force. That head of yours should be of use as well as ornament."

Holmes later brings off a dazzling *coup de théâtre* as, before the two police inspectors' unsuspecting eyes, he captures the cab-driver murderer after having lured him to 221B Baker Street on the pretence of picking up a customer. The text then turns into a third-person narrative relating events dating back to 1847 in the American wilderness that have culminated in the revenge murder of Enoch J. Drebber in London. This stodgy, dispensable, and controversial representation of

Mormon history occupies a full third of the text before Watson is allowed to continue his reminiscences, in which the murderer confesses to his work in London and Holmes explains how he reasoned out the case. The police take all the credit in the press for apprehending the criminal, but Watson promises to publish the true account and display Holmes's achievements.

Here then, in this very first story, are the Holmes/Watson relationship and the pattern for later stories fully established. Watson displays himself as a simple man, prepared to make a fool of himself (and tell stories against himself), slow to understand Holmes's methods and ever ready to forgive his shortcomings as a human being. Watson's ordinariness contrasts with Holmes's cold, intellectual near-infallibility.

A Study in Scarlet is important for giving us the only full description of Holmes.

> His very person and appearance were such as to strike the attention of the most casual observer. In height he was rather over six feet, and so excessively lean that he seemed to be considerably taller. His eyes were sharp and piercing . . . and his thin, hawk-like nose gave his whole expression an air of alertness and decision. His chin, too, had the prominence and squareness which mark the man of determination . . . he was possessed of extraordinary delicacy of touch . . .

This description forms one basis for judging the success of the artists and actors who have shown us Sherlock Holmes. Of Watson, we know from Stamford's description that he is "thin as a lath and as brown as a nut", but of course, this thinness may be a temporary state attributable to his poor health. The story also provides the only description of the Baker Street rooms: "They consisted of a couple of comfortable bedrooms and a single large airy sitting-room, cheerfully furnished, and illuminated by two broad windows." (No mention of a bathroom is ever made in any of the Sherlock Holmes stories.) There are references to "the landlady", but she is not as yet identified as Mrs Hudson.

The story is far less interesting than the characterization of Sherlock Holmes. It has some very awkward developments; it is hard, for instance, to accept that Holmes could be fooled by a young man dressed up as an old lady, or that the murderer returned to the same Baker Street address that his mysterious accomplice had earlier visited. And the Mormon flashback commonly ranks as the least favourite episode among devotees of the Sherlock Holmes stories.

Conan Doyle makes an odd acknowledgement to the inspiration provided by previous fictional detectives. He has Watson tell Holmes, "You remind me of Edgar Allan Poe's Dupin." But he then has Holmes dismiss Dupin as "a very inferior fellow", prompting Watson to ask his opinion of Emile Gaboriau's Monsieur Lecoq. Holmes is even more dismissive:

> Lecoq was a miserable bungler; he had only one thing to recommend him and that was his energy. That book made me positively ill. The question was how to identify an unknown prisoner. I could have done it in twenty-four hours. Lecoq took six months or so. It might be made a text-book for detectives to teach them what to avoid.

Of course, Holmes rarely had any respect for other detectives, but it does make a reader wonder whether Conan Doyle shared the same view. When in 1912 Arthur Guiterman published a poem chiding Conan Doyle for being less than candid over his indebtedness to Poe and Gaboriau, the reply, titled *To An Undiscerning Critic*, was wittily composed:

> He, the created, would scoff and would sneer,
> Where I, the creator, would bow and revere.
> So please grip this fact with your cerebral tentacle:
> The doll and its maker are never identical.

The murderer tries to escape through the window after he is apprehended at Baker Street in *A Study in Scarlet*. Lestrade and Holmes prevent him succeeding in George Hutchinson's frontispiece to the 1891 edition.

MORE HOLMES
THE SIGN OF FOUR
AND THE TWELVE ADVENTURES

While he was working on *A Study in Scarlet*, Conan Doyle was also planning a historical novel, *Micah Clarke*, which required substantial research into the 17th century. Conan Doyle's ambition was to rival Sir Walter Scott and Robert Louis Stevenson, and it was as a historical novelist that he wanted to make his literary reputation. He sold *Micah Clarke* to Longmans, Green and received a standard 10 per cent royalty. Its immediate success encouraged him to start work on another historical opus, this time set in the 14th century and demanding more research.

In August 1889, however, he was invited to a dinner by J. M. Stoddart, who recruited him and another guest, Oscar Wilde, to write for the American *Lippincott's Monthly Magazine*. As a result, Wilde wrote *The Picture of Dorian Gray* and Conan Doyle revived Sherlock Holmes for another story, which he had completed by early October. *The Sign of the Four* appeared (unillustrated) in *Lippincott's* February 1890 issue, published both in America and England. When it was issued in book form, its title was modified to *The Sign of Four* and it had a single illustration, depicting Sherlock Holmes.

In *A Study in Scarlet*, Watson wrote of weeks when Holmes lay on the sofa: "On these occasions I have noticed such a dreamy, vacant expression in his eyes, that I might have suspected him of being addicted to the use of some narcotic, had not the temperance and cleanliness of his whole life forbidden such a notion." In *The Sign of Four*, Watson is beginning to know Holmes better, and his account opens with the detective's three-times-a-day indulgence in a seven-per-cent solution of cocaine. Holmes recognizes that it is a bad habit (although it was not then illegal):

> I find it, however, so transcendently stimulating and clarifying to the mind that its secondary action is a matter of small moment. . . . My mind rebels at stagnation. Give me problems, give me work, give me the most abstruse cryptogram, or the most intricate analysis, and I am in my own proper atmosphere. I can dispense then with artificial stimulants.

In *The Sign of Four* there are positive statements by Holmes regarding women and romance. "It is of first importance not to allow your judgment to be biased by personal qualities," he states, and he fails to notice the attractiveness of his young client, Mary Morstan. (Or is Watson biased, being smitten with her at first sight, and wooing and winning her for his wife by the end of the story?) When Miss Morstan falters in describing her father's disappearance, Holmes offers no sympathy but simply asks when it happened. He is later complimentary towards her, but only as a budding detective! For him, "Women are never to be entirely trusted – not the best of them". And also, "love is an emotional thing, and whatever is emotional is opposed to that true cold reason which I place above all things. I should never marry myself, lest I bias my judgment."

The trail leads to a house called Pondicherry Lodge in Norwood, where the body of one Bartholomew Sholto is found behind a locked door. It is a mystery to which Holmes applies his famous maxim: "when you have eliminated the impossible, whatever remains, *however improbable*, must be the truth." After having been taken in by a disguise in *A Study in Scarlet*, Holmes this time masquerades as a wheezy old sea salt, and turns up at Baker Street, fooling both Watson and Scotland Yard's Inspector Athelney Jones. Holmes declares that he has to disguise himself now that

This is the only illustration – by Charles Kerr – that was used as a frontispiece to *The Sign of Four* when it appeared as a book in 1890. It portrays the moment when Sherlock Holmes hands to Watson the note that he has found by the body of Benjamin Sholto at Pondicherry Lodge. Holmes appears to have a moustache!

Watson has made him so famous by his writings. There is an exciting climax, a vividly written chase down the Thames, in which (for the only recorded time) Holmes fires his gun at a human target, the pygmy Tonga.

Like *A Study in Scarlet*, *The Sign of Four* incorporates a long account of ancient treachery on another continent that has prompted the events in London, but it is not such a substantial interruption as the Mormon episode, and it is better written. There is an earlier short account in which Mary Morstan explains the occurrences that have brought her to see Sherlock Holmes, and this sets the pattern for later stories in which characters present their problems to the detective with little or no recorded interruption from him.

Arthur Conan Doyle finished his new historical novel, *The White Company*, in July 1890. The following month he took off for the International Medical Congress in Berlin and, as a result, decided to set up in London as an ophthalmologist. He and his wife moved from Southsea in December 1890. He spent some time struggling to study the human eye in Vienna, and then set himself up as a consultant at 2 Devonshire Place in central London. *The White Company* was published in 12 monthly instalments in the *Cornhill Magazine* from January 1891, and it was also issued in book form that year. Although it was the work that its author regarded with the most pride, it is choked by its attention to period detail and the use of archaic language; it has few literary admirers today.

The launch of *The Strand Magazine* provided Conan Doyle with a new outlet, and the magazine's policy of running complete short stories with recurring characters

SIX PENCE

THE STRAND MAGAZINE

BURLEIGH STREET

359

EDITED
By
Geo. Newnes

OFFICES

Nº 7
VOL. 2

JULY
1891

AN·ILLUSTRATED·MONTHLY

instead of serializing novels gave him the idea of reviving Sherlock Holmes in more reminiscences by his companion, Doctor Watson. In his many unoccupied moments at Devonshire Place, he wrote two short stories that so delighted the magazine's editor, Herbert Greenhough Smith, that four more were commissioned, and the six stories ran in consecutive issues of the *Strand* from July 1891. The first stories caused such a sensation that Conan Doyle had to write six further cases by the end of the year so that the magazine could continue to feature Holmes each month until its June 1892 issue. Already, however, the author was beginning to resent the commercial pressures that were being brought to bear on him, and he wrote to his mother that he would kill off Sherlock Holmes after the 12 stories. He did, however, feel confident enough to abandon his work as an eye specialist in favour of a literary career, and he bought a large house at 12 Tennison Road, South Norwood, the area of London that Holmes had visited in *The Sign of Four*.

To illustrate the *Strand* stories, the magazine's art editor chose Walter Paget but his brother Sidney was commissioned by mistake. However, the tall, good-looking

Opposite is the cover of *The Strand Magazine* which published the first of the Sherlock Holmes short stories for which it became famous. This was *A Scandal in Bohemia*. The drawing is of the Strand looking towards Fleet Street. (Photographed in the Stanley Mackenzie Collection.)

In this letter to his mother dated 11 November 1891 (left), Conan Doyle mentions his intention of killing Holmes after only six short stories. Above, he is seen with his wife Louise outside the house at 12 Tennison Road, South Norwood. The house still stands and bears a plaque commemorating his stay there.

SHERLOCK HOLMES A CENTENARY CELEBRATION

Opposite are three of Sidney Paget's drawings for the first story, *A Scandal in Bohemia*. Left is a cosy domestic scene at Baker Street as Holmes warms himself by the fire and chats to Watson. Right, Holmes, in his disguise as a clergyman, is about to enter 221B Baker Street with Watson when Irene Adler, dressed up as a young man, calls out "Good night, Mister Sherlock Holmes". Holmes cannot place who it is. This is the only occasion on which Paget depicted the outside of Holmes's quarters. Below right, while following Irene Adler in another disguise, Holmes (front left) is roped in as a witness to her wedding.

Walter served as Sidney's model for Sherlock Holmes, and the artist took Conan Doyle as his inspiration for Watson. The engravers handled Paget's drawings with varying skill, and so there are inconsistencies in the depiction of the two characters in the actual magazine. Overall Holmes was represented as a dashingly attractive figure – which helped immeasurably in making him so popular. This was not how Conan Doyle envisaged Holmes: he should have been a "more beaky nosed, hawk-faced man", rather ugly and cadaverous-looking. Again, Conan Doyle had the feeling that he was losing control of his creation. . . .

The first short story, *A Scandal in Bohemia*, is memorable for featuring the one woman whom Holmes comes to admire. Irene Adler is not a villain, but she possesses an incriminating photograph from a liaison with the King of Bohemia and threatens to wreck his proposed marriage. Holmes is shown at his most theatrical: he adopts two disguises and stages an elaborate piece of street theatre, with at least a dozen hired hands, to gain access to Irene Adler's home. Miss Adler outwits him at every turn: she fools him by masquerading as a youth and impudently wishes him

The brothers Paget. Artists both, it was Walter (above) who served as the model for Sherlock Holmes when his brother Sidney (left) began illustrating the stories in the *Strand*. Sidney Paget depicted scenes in 38 adventures, including *The Hound of the Baskervilles*. After Sidney's early death, Walter illustrated one story.

good night in the street, then just as coolly leaves a message for him and a portrait of herself in the former hiding place of the prized photograph. Holmes goes so far as to describe her as "a lovely woman, with a face that a man might die for", and he keeps her photograph as a precious souvenir. The King admires her also. "Is it not a pity that she was not on my level?" he asks, and Holmes replies, "From what I have seen of the lady she seems indeed to be on a very different level to your Majesty." Holmes delights in her style and resourcefulness: for him, she is always *the* woman.

The Red-Headed League introduces a strange organization that apparently benefits red-haired men. Holmes's client, Jabez Wilson, has been handsomely paid to attend a bare office and copy out by hand the *Encyclopaedia Britannica* for eight weeks. It is our good fortune that he is concerned enough at the sudden dissolution of the League to consult Holmes, who finds the circumstances piquant – "quite a three pipe problem". The solution is prosaic but dramatic.

A Case of Identity brings Miss Mary Sutherland to Baker Street with a tale of a vanished fiancé called Hosmer Angel, a "trite" problem which Holmes solves without having to leave the premises. The culprit is one of the most despicable figures in the canon. "The law cannot, as you say, touch you yet there never was a man who deserved punishment more," Holmes tells the unrepentant scoundrel and comes close to horse-whipping him. A surprising number of other cases do not feature crime in the legal sense.

In *The Boscombe Valley Mystery*, Holmes and Watson take the train to Herefordshire to investigate the murder of one Charles McCarthy. For the journey

Holmes is described as wearing "his long grey travelling-cloak and close-fitting cloth cap", and it was Sidney Paget who chose to depict him wearing a deerstalker cap, the headgear that Paget himself wore in the country. It was therefore Paget, not Conan Doyle, who contributed this key feature of Holmes's image. Inspector Lestrade reappears on this case and is quickly bemused by Holmes's approach. "I find it hard enough to tackle facts, Mr Holmes, without flying away after theories and fancies," he says, leaving Holmes to reply demurely, "You do find it very hard to tackle the facts." It is an absorbing case, with all the clues that enable Holmes to reach the truth being clearly presented. Holmes chooses not to expose the murderer because of the extenuating circumstances and because the man has not long to live.

At one stage in the next story, *The Five Orange Pips*, Watson reports Holmes "more depressed and shaken than I had ever seen him". His client, John Openshaw, has fallen victim to the long arm of the Ku Klux Klan, which seeks revenge for a betrayal in America. Holmes makes a special point of arranging retribution, but his plans are foiled by circumstances beyond his control. In itself, it is an unsatisfying case to read, but the occasional upset makes the cases more varied and true to life.

By a happy chance, in *The Man with the Twisted Lip*, Watson crosses Holmes's path while the detective is disguised as an old man in an opium den and is invited to follow the rest of the case. Holmes locates the missing Neville St Clair who has a secret so grave that, rather than reveal it to his wife, he stands falsely accused of murder. The case is distinctive because Holmes never explains how he solved it; the story is already longer than most, and perhaps Conan Doyle ran out of space. Some indication of the haste and disregard for consistency with which he wrote these stories ("Sherlock Holmes takes my mind from better things", he complained) may

A villain pleads for mercy and confesses all. Holmes, seen in a God-like position, decides that he has learned a lesson and spares him as it is the season of goodwill. Sidney Paget provided this illustration for the Christmas story, *The Adventure of the Blue Carbuncle* (*Strand*, January 1892 issue).

be gleaned from the fact that Watson's wife calls him James rather than John.

There is a festive flavouring to *The Adventure of the Blue Carbuncle* to tie in with its appearance in the Christmas number of *The Strand Magazine*. It begins with an apparently trivial incident – a mislaid hat and Christmas goose that a commissionaire picked up after a street brawl – but in the goose is hidden a missing precious stone, the Blue Carbuncle. Holmes tracks down the guilty party and, out of seasonal generosity perhaps, lets him off, even though it will delay the release of someone else wrongly accused. There is a reward of £1,000 for recovering the Blue Carbuncle, which, one hopes, Holmes shared with the commissionaire.

The Adventure of the Speckled Band is one of the best-remembered of all the stories. In it Sherlock Holmes turns the tables on the dastardly Dr Grimesby Roylott. Here is one of the most striking villains in the canon, bursting into the Baker Street sitting room and backing up his threats to Holmes by twisting a steel poker into a curve. After his visitor's departure, Holmes calmly straightens out the poker and remarks to Watson, "The incident gives zest to our investigation." It is a complex and scary affair.

Doctor Watson next records one of the only two cases he introduced to Holmes's attention. (The other concerned the madness of Colonel Warburton, which is among the many unpublished adventures to which tantalising reference is made – part of a clever storytelling touch by Conan Doyle to suggest the volume of work at 221B). The case in point is *The Adventure of the Engineer's Thumb*, which concerned a thumb that was severed from the hand of hydraulic engineer Victor Hatherley at the end of a strange business trip to the Reading area for a certain Colonel Lysander Stark. Holmes's sole deduction is that the distance Hatherley travelled away from

Sherlock Holmes invites Watson to study an old and battered felt hat for information about its owner. Watson can read nothing, and Holmes amazes his friend by the amount he has extracted from the object. Another of Sidney Paget's illustrations for *The Adventure of the Blue Carbuncle* (it is signed also by the engravers).

Reading station was faked. Even the police realize that a gang of counterfeiters is behind the incident, and the conclusion is another of the unsatisfactory but lifelike variety. The villains get clean away and Watson records that "even Holmes's ingenuity failed ever to discover the least clue to their whereabouts".

In *The Adventure of the Noble Bachelor*, we find well demonstrated Holmes's commendable dislike of snobbery: when the impoverished aristocrat Lord Robert St Simon indicates that Holmes should feel privileged to be consulted by a man of his rank, the detective is able to reply that his last aristocratic client was the King of Scandinavia (another untold story). Holmes clearly prefers the honest American

Holmes points a pistol at a villain's head in *The Adventure of the Beryl Coronet* and extracts from him the whereabouts of some missing gems. Sidney Paget's illustration appeared in the *Strand*'s May 1892 issue.

Holmes lashes out at the hissing intruder slithering down the bell-pull in the darkened bedroom at the climax of *The Adventure of the Speckled Band*, illustrated by Sidney Paget for the *Strand*, February 1892.

who lured St Simon's wife away from her wedding breakfast. Holmes tells him:

> It is always a joy to meet an American, Mr Moulton, for I am one of those who believe that the folly of a monarch and the blundering of a minister in far-gone years will not prevent our children from being some day citizens of the same world-wide country under a flag which shall be a quartering of the Union Jack with the Stars and Stripes.

Americans feature prominently in many stories, although if this was intended to enhance the appeal of the cases in the United States, it is surprising how many of them are unsavoury villains.

Sherlock Holmes is a practical man, and in *The Adventure of the Beryl Coronet* he shows that he is willing to make deals with the criminal world when it is the most sensible way to resolve a case. Here, after an investigation in which he disguises himself as a layabout to glean information, he pays £3,000 to a fence to recover a priceless piece of jewellery, and takes an additional £1,000 as his reward for returning them to the unfortunate banker who is responsible for their safety.

Conan Doyle's mother is reputed to have given him the idea for the last of the 12 stories, *The Adventure of the Copper Beeches*, in which Holmes is discovered in a sour mood occasioned by lack of activity. He criticizes Watson for his unscientific accounts of his cases and despairs when his advice is first sought by Miss Violet Hunter on whether she should accept a position as a governess in Hampshire. But her account of the unusually high salary, the curious conditions and the light duties, lead him to devise seven separate (and unrevealed) explanations in the absence of more data. Not for the first time in these stories, the villain is a father or step-father fearful of losing access to a daughter's private income if she marries. Jephro Rucastle is one of the most colourful scoundrels of the sagas, a hearty storyteller who threatens to loose on Miss Hunter the famished mastiff he keeps locked away. Watson is disappointed that Holmes took no further interest in Miss Hunter after the case was satisfactorily concluded, for she was evidently another woman who took the good doctor's Bohemian eye.

Sidney Paget depicts a recurring scene in the stories: Sherlock Holmes listens intently, fingertips touching, as a client outlines the problem. Here the visitor is Violet Hunter who is worried about the unusual conditions attached to a job as a governess. The story is *The Adventure of the Copper Beeches* (*Strand*, June 1892).

Before this set of adventures had been concluded in *The Strand Magazine*, Conan Doyle had committed himself to writing a further dozen stories when the publishers agreed to meet his high asking price of £1,000. However, he first wrote an historical novel about the Napoleonic era, *The Great Shadow*, which was published in October 1892, the same month that his 12 Sherlock Holmes short stories appeared in book form as *The Adventures of Sherlock Holmes* (the British publishers used all 104 of the illustrations Paget had drawn for the *Strand*, while the American edition used only 16). Conan Doyle dedicated the English edition to "My old teacher, Joseph Bell, M.D.", and Bell was invited to review it in the magazine *Bookman*. He wrote of Conan Doyle's "well-deserved success" and emphasized how Sherlock Holmes's methods were similar to those of medical diagnosis and how his deductions might encourage the reader to observe more things himself. Bell's own observations led him to describe Conan Doyle as "a born story-teller":

> He has had the wit to devise excellent plots, interesting complications; he tells them in honest Saxon-English with directness and pith; and, above all his other merits, his stories are absolutely free from padding. He knows how delicious brevity is, how everything tends to be too long, and he has given us stories that we can read at a sitting between dinner and coffee, and we have not a chance to forget the beginning before we reach the end. The ordinary detective story, from Gaboriau or Boisgobey down to the latest shocker, really needs an effort of memory quite misplaced to keep the circumstances of the crimes and all the wrong scents of the various meddlers before the wearied reader.

Joseph Bell was an observant literary critic as well.

MORE MEMOIRS OF SHERLOCK HOLMES

Conan Doyle wrote three new Sherlock Holmes cases during the summer of 1892. Publication began in the *Strand*'s December 1892 number, and the new series of 11 adventures ended in the December 1893 issue, with one, *The Adventure of the Naval Treaty*, being spread over two months. Sidney Paget again supplied all the *Strand*'s illustrations. Most of the stories were acquired for American publication by *Harper's Weekly*, which engaged W. H. Hyde to provide one or two illustrations for each. Various British and American newspapers also printed the stories before they were issued in book form as *The Memoirs of Sherlock Holmes*.

Paget again depicted Sherlock Holmes in deerstalker and long travelling cape on the train journey with Watson to Dartmoor in the first of these new cases, *The Adventure of Silver Blaze*. A famous racehorse, Silver Blaze, has disappeared days before a big race and his trainer lies dead. It is one of the most memorable of the tales, not only for its unusual solution, but for the famous passage in which Inspector Gregory fishes for Holmes's help:

"Is there any point to which you would wish to draw my attention?"
"To the curious incident of the dog in the night-time."
"The dog did nothing in the night-time."
"That was the curious incident," remarked Sherlock Holmes.

One of Sidney Paget's most celebrated illustrations from the *Strand* (December 1892 issue), this shows Holmes and Watson *en route* to the West Country to investigate the disappearance of the racehorse in *The Adventure of Silver Blaze*. The deerstalker and cape were Holmes's regular attire for cases that took him to the country.

What the dog didn't do is as important as what he did, and his failure to raise the alarm when Silver Blaze was removed from the stable proves significant. Because Silver Blaze's owner has been "a trifle cavalier" towards Holmes, the detective delays revealing that the animal is safe and well and running in the big race. Holmes further teases him when revealing the identity of the killer.

The Adventure of the Cardboard Box opens with a celebrated mind-reading episode, in which Holmes demonstrates to Watson that Poe was not exaggerating when he described a similar feat. The cardboard box contains two freshly severed ears, and Holmes (who has written articles about the human ear) has no difficulty in discovering why they were sent to a Croydon spinster before he allows Inspector Lestrade to again take all the credit. Here is a stark instance of domestic strife: a man has killed his wife and her lover and sent their ears to the sister-in-law who is behind all his troubles. Haunted by his crime, the murderer is in mental agony, and Holmes offers a rare philosophical deliberation that Watson quotes to close the tale:

> What is the meaning of it, Watson? What object is served by this circle of misery and violence and fear? It must tend to some end, or else our universe is ruled by chance, which is unthinkable. But what end? There is the great standing perennial problem to which human reason is as far from an answer as ever.

The Adventure of the Yellow Face brings Grant Munro to Baker Street. He wishes to consult Sherlock Holmes over the mysterious conduct of his wife, who has been sneaking off to a neighbouring cottage where a livid yellow face has been observed looking out of a window. Holmes is convinced that the wife is being blackmailed and supports the husband's decision to force his way into the cottage illegally. All ends happily after Holmes discovers that his supposition is entirely wrong; and he humbly retreats from the scene. Disappointingly slight in itself, the case does widen

Sherlock Holmes visits Watson at his Paddington surgery and has soon recruited his company for *The Adventure of the Stockbroker's Clerk*. This Sidney Paget illustration is from the *Strand*'s March 1893 issue. Holmes's headgear is more suitable for wearing around town than the deerstalker. Paget is often quite grudging about background detail, as here.

our understanding of Holmes by showing him making a mistake, while our respec for him is enhanced by his willingness to acknowledge it.

The Adventure of the Stockbroker's Clerk features a clerk, Hall Pycroft, who has been lured to Birmingham and employed on a rather pointless time-consuming task. The plot is patterned after that of *The Red-Headed League* and suffers a fundamental weakness in having a prominent financial house, whose premises hold valuable securities, employ a clerk on the basis of his letter of application without interviewing him.

Conan Doyle next wrote two stories that give us rare glimpses of the young Sherlock Holmes at work before he met Doctor Watson. In both instances, Sherlock Holmes interests Watson with souvenirs of the cases and then describes what happened, so that they are essentially told by Holmes rather than by the good doctor.

In *The Adventure of the "Gloria Scott"*, Holmes goes on holiday to Norfolk to visit the father of Victor Trevor, his only college friend. He astounds and alarms the older Trevor by the details he discerns of the man's past from his appearance and gains the compliment, "I don't know how you manage this, Mr Holmes, but it seems to me that all the detectives of fact and of fancy would be children in your hands. That's your line of life, sir, and you may take the word of a man who has seen something of the world." It encourages Holmes to think that his powers might be turned into a profession. But after old Trevor's past tragically catches up with him, Holmes loses the son's friendship when he goes far away to forget the incident.

This is how Sidney Paget showed the young Sherlock Holmes on his very first case while a university graduate. He is studying the coded message that has brought such consternation to his friend's father in *The Adventure of the "Gloria Scott"* (*Strand*, April 1893).

Holmes also recalls *The Adventure of the Musgrave Ritual*, which was the third case that he investigated after setting up in practice as a consulting detective. He was flattered to be engaged by the aristocratic Reginald Musgrave to look into strange happenings at the manor house of Hurlstone. Holmes solved the meaning of the old catechism called the Musgrave Ritual, and the case provides a rare opening for Conan Doyle's passion for history when an ancient crown of the Kings of England is revealed to be at the heart of the matter. Quite apart from the intricacy of the problem, this story is prized for the opening description of the chaotic state of the sitting room at 221B Baker Street. The chaos is due not only to Holmes's untidiness ("month after month his papers accumulated, until every corner of the room was stacked with bundles of manuscript which were on no account to be burned") but to his eccentricities, including his habit of putting bullet holes that form a patriotic "V.R." (for Victoria Regina) into the wall for target practice (causing Watson to remark, "I felt strongly that neither the atmosphere nor the appearance of our room was improved by it").

In *The Adventure of the Reigate Squire*, Holmes is taken by Watson to Reigate in Surrey to recuperate from the strain of defeating "the most accomplished swindler in Europe" (one of the unrecorded cases). But he recovers his health investigating a local mystery, although he feigns physical and mental fatigue for good reasons and fools Watson. It seems unlikely that one of the two murderers would have retained

incriminating evidence in his dressing-gown or that this pair would be so mistrustful of each other to share the writing of a note. This story was published in America as *The Reigate Puzzle* and is also known as *The Adventure of the Reigate Squires*.

The Adventure of the Crooked Man shows Sherlock Holmes arriving just before midnight at Watson's residence a few months after the doctor's marriage to request his company on a trip to Aldershot the following day. Does Holmes actually yearn for the companionship of his old flatmate? He says that he needs Watson's support in confronting a dangerous-looking individual who holds the key to an apparent murder. An account of past betrayal in India during the Mutiny is unfurled, and Holmes is satisfied that no killing actually took place. At the beginning of this case, Holmes correctly deduces from Watson's appearance that he is professionally busy and shrugs off Watson's applause by declaring that it was "elementary". In *The Adventure of the Cardboard Box*, Holmes read Watson's thoughts and, after explaining how it was done, adds, "It was very superficial, my dear Watson, I assure you." Nowhere in the canon does Holmes utter the phrase "Elementary, my dear Watson" in one piece.

Young Percy Trevelyan of *The Adventure of the Resident Patient* is a medical specialist who has found the success that eluded the young Conan Doyle in London. He owes his start to the financial backing of a mysterious figure called Blessington, who becomes his resident patient. Blessington seeks Holmes's help when his room

Above, at the beginning of *The Adventure of the Musgrave Ritual*, Sherlock Holmes brings out the large tin box with mementoes of his early cases, extracts the relics of that particular investigation, his first as a professional detective, and then describes it to Watson. Above left, the young consultant is seen working out the solution to the Musgrave ritual, which leads him to the cellar underneath the stone-flagged floor. These Paget illustrations first appeared in the *Strand* for May 1893.

is disturbed but is refused because he won't reveal why he is in danger. Holmes knows that he fears for his life, and when Blessington is murdered the same night we may feel that the detective should have helped him. But Holmes is able to reconstruct the crime mentally from the information in the dead man's room – footprints, cigar ash and so forth. As in *The Red-Headed League* and *The Stockbroker's Clerk*, the villains display considerable ingenuity, here posing as Russian noblemen and faking catalepsy, but the crime behind it all is rather commonplace.

The most memorable feature of *The Adventure of the Greek Interpreter* is the introduction of Sherlock's brother, Mycroft. Although Mycroft is even more gifted at observation and deduction, he lacks the ambition and energy to rival his younger brother. Watson has not previously known of Mycroft's existence, and even now Holmes withholds the significance of the work that Mycroft carries out for the British government. Mycroft passes on to Sherlock the case of the Greek interpreter. It is not one of his most successful investigations, as the interpreter nearly loses his life and the villains escape from his clutches after killing their prisoner.

Right, Mycroft sits in the Baker Street rooms, awaiting the return of his brother, Sherlock, and Watson in *The Adventure of the Greek Interpreter*, which was illustrated by Sidney Paget in the September 1893 *Strand*. Below, Holmes's odd sense of humour and love of theatrical touch are evident at the conclusion of *The Adventure of the Naval Treaty* when the detective returns the missing papers to his client on a platter at the breakfast table. The November 1893 *Strand* carried this Paget drawing.

The longest of all the short stories is *The Adventure of the Naval Treaty*. An old schoolfriend of Watson's, Percy Phelps, who has become a Whitehall clerk, loses a precious treaty he is copying, which is removed from his desk late one night. Why did the thief draw attention to his presence by ringing the bell to call the commissionaire? Holmes sets an elaborate trap and catches the guilty party in the act of recovering the stolen document from its hiding place.

Reaching the last of the 12 stories he had agreed to write, Arthur Conan Doyle was so weary of being identified with Sherlock Holmes and what he regarded as "a lower stratum of literary achievement" that he carried out his threats to do away with the great detective. In *The Adventure of the Final Problem*, Conan Doyle introduces Professor James Moriarty, "the Napoleon of crime", whom Holmes has identified just four months previously as "the organizer of half that is evil and of nearly all that is undetected in this great city."

SP

The evil Professor Moriarty takes his leave after visiting Holmes at Baker Street in *The Adventure of the Final Problem*. The encounter has featured in many plays and films. This is how Sidney Paget visualized it in the December 1893 *Strand*.

The two respect each other as intellectual equals. "My horror at his crimes was lost in my admiration at his skill," Holmes tells Watson. They have physical similarities, both being tall, thin and with prominent foreheads. There is a memorable scene in which Moriarty visits Holmes at Baker Street and the pair meet for the first time. Moriarty warns Holmes: "If you are clever enough to bring destruction upon me, rest assured that I shall do as much to you." Holmes responds: ". . . if I were assured of the former eventuality I would, in the interests of the public, cheerfully accept the latter."

Holmes's elaborate attempts to remove himself from Moriarty's clutches fail, and there is the final confrontation, on a narrow path in Switzerland overlooking the 300-foot high Reichenbach Falls, that one senses Holmes really desires, as he has allowed Watson to be decoyed away. Moriarty charitably allows his foe to write a farewell message to the good doctor, who concludes that the two men plunged to their deaths locked in each other's arms. It is a clean, swift end with no bodies being recovered and no distressing details to dwell on.

Although it is not the first such ending in the stories (the villains of *The Five Orange Pips* were presumed to have drowned at sea), in the circumstances here it makes an appropriately spectacular conclusion to the great detective's career. And, of course, the absence of his body left the possibility that Sherlock Holmes had somehow survived. Even so, contemporary readers assumed the worst. Some were so dismayed that they wore black mourning bands, others wrote angry and abusive letters to Conan Doyle, who records in his autobiography: "I was amazed at the concern expressed by the public. They say that a man is never properly appreciated until he is dead, and the general protest against my summary execution of Holmes taught me how many and how numerous were his friends . . ."

This last group of stories, with the exception of *The Adventure of the Cardboard Box*, has appeared in book form in both Britain and the United States as *The Memoirs of Sherlock Holmes*. On reflection, Conan Doyle regarded *The Adventure of the Cardboard Box* as too sensational, but he rated the opening thought-reading episode highly and crudely inserted it into the beginning of *The Adventure of the*

Resident Patient so that it carried contradictory references to a blazing hot day in October. In the process, readers have been denied a small but pleasing vignette of Baker Street life:

> It was boisterous October weather, and we had both remained indoors all day, I because I feared with my shaken health to face the keen autumn wind, while he was deep in some of those abstruse chemical investigations which absorbed him utterly as long as he was engaged upon them. Towards evening, however, the breaking of a test-tube brought his research to a premature ending, and he sprang up from his chair with an exclamation of impatience and a clouded brow.
>
> "A day's work ruined, Watson," said he, striding across to the window. "Ha! the stars are out and the wind has fallen. What do you say to a ramble through London?"

The decrepit Italian priest in the railway carriage fools Watson – it is another of Holmes's disguises, here part of his attempt to elude Moriarty in *The Adventure of the Final Problem*. Illustration by Sidney Paget in the *Strand* for December 1893.

Opposite, Good and Evil are locked in deadly combat at the Reichenbach Falls in Paget's vivid whole page illustration for *The Adventure of the Final Problem*. Paget unusually signed his name in full – perhaps because the work was larger than most, he took particular pride in it, and it was the last illustration he expected to draw of Sherlock Holmes.

SHERLOCK HOLMES ON STAGE

Having done away with Holmes, or so he thought, Arthur Conan Doyle was able to concentrate on the higher stratum of historical fiction. He provided *The Strand Magazine* with a series of Brigadier Gerard stories for the issues from April to December 1895. These vividly evoke the colourful Napoleonic era. In 1896, the *Strand* ran in 12 parts his boxing story *Rodney Stone*. In book form, his recent work appeared in 1896 as *The Exploits of Brigadier Gerard* and as *Rodney Stone*. Other books followed.

Holmes and Watson were briefly revived but only as Conan Doyle's contribution to a special issue of the Edinburgh University student journal, to be sold at a bazaar to help raise funds for a new sports pavilion. *The Field Bazaar* has Holmes read that Watson's mind is preoccupied with a request to help the bazaar and conclude correctly that Watson will use this latest demonstration of his powers as the subject for a literary contribution.

Conan Doyle had become interested in writing for the theatre, but his efforts – whether in collaboration, adapting his own work, or adapting the work of another novelist – had not made a great impression. Realizing that he would have more chance of being successful if he wrote a play featuring Sherlock Holmes, in late 1897 or early 1898 he devised a story from the sleuth's early career that also featured Professor Moriarty. This provided two plum parts likely to attract the big stage names of the day. The celebrated Herbert Beerbohm Tree was interested but wanted too many changes.

The project appealed to the prominent Broadway impresario Charles Frohman, who persuaded Conan Doyle that the American stage star William Gillette would be ideal casting for Sherlock Holmes. Gillette was also a successful playwright, and, attired in deerstalker cap and flowing cape, he visited Conan Doyle to seek permission to perform the part and to reshape the play to make it more acceptable to American playgoers.

Conan Doyle was initially unhappy about the planned introduction of such traditional ingredients as a love interest for Holmes, but in later years, after the play's success, he was fond of recounting how he had received a cable from Gillette in America asking "May I marry Holmes?" to which he responded: "You may marry him, murder him, or do anything you like with him." It seems most likely that Conan Doyle had given up trying to influence Gillette's activities a whole continent away, but he maintained that his reply demonstrated unqualified confidence in the American.

After studying the existing stories, Gillette built up his play, *Sherlock Holmes*, from *A Scandal in Bohemia* and *The Final Problem* with bits and pieces from other cases and some fresh material. Conan Doyle very properly received co-author credit because so much of the plot and dialogue was his, but its adaptation for the stage was entirely Gillette's work, as Conan Doyle has clearly stated. The play opened in New York on 6 November 1899 for a successful run before Gillette brought it to London's Lyceum Theatre (an appropriate choice, because it had featured in *The Sign of Four*) for another lengthy engagement from 9 September 1901.

From *A Scandal in Bohemia*, Gillette took Holmes's task of recovering evidence of a past love affair to prevent scandal, but he discarded Irene Adler, introducing instead the sweet young Alice Faulkner who is intent on avenging a dead sister. The

William Gillette (1856–1937) became inseparably identified with the role of Sherlock Holmes in both Britain and America.

William Gillette as the great detective is seen at Baker Street in Act One Scene Three of his play *Sherlock Holmes*. He is issuing instructions to one of his helpers, Terese, the maid in the household where Alice Faulkner is virtually a prisoner.

A poster for the first London production of the William Gillette play in 1901–2, and below, an artist's impression of the celebrated meeting of Holmes and Moriarty at Baker Street, as recreated in the play.

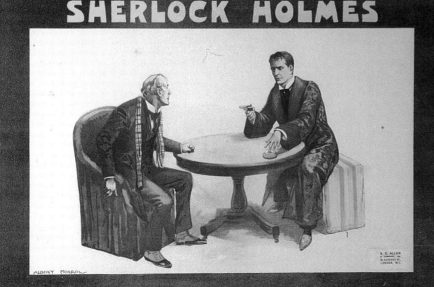

Right, a poster for the London production, showing William Gillette in the gas chamber scene, has been adapted for use by Ben Greet's company, which took the play on tour at the end of 1901 with various actors playing the detective.

problem for Holmes is to persuade Alice to return the mementoes voluntarily and give up her plan. Holmes adopts the rather devious strategy of encouraging her to fall in love with him so that she returns the items to save his career from apparent ruin. (If this seems uncharacteristically callous, it should be remembered that in a later story, *The Adventure of Charles Augustus Milverton*, Conan Doyle had Holmes woo a housemaid called Agatha to gain information and he even became engaged to her – although this is not described in any detail and Watson rightly disapproves on hearing about it.) This stage Holmes does, however, repent of his tactics, and he refuses to accept the package from Alice, which convinces her that he must really

This fine cartoon of William Gillette as Sherlock Holmes by "Spy" (Leslie Ward) appeared in a supplement to *Vanity Fair* in 1907 as part of a series called "Men of the Day".

care about her. And so he does, replying, "Your powers of observation are somewhat remarkable, Miss Faulkner . . . and your deduction is quite correct! I suppose . . . indeed I know . . . that I love you." As he embraces her, the curtain falls. Despite Conan Doyle's consent, Gillette does not go quite so far as to marry Holmes. Still, this is a shattering enough depiction of the man who (to quote Watson in *A Scandal in Bohemia*) "never spoke of the softer emotions save with a gibe and a sneer".

Gillette incorporated the great confrontation scene between Holmes and Moriarty from *The Final Problem*, but he slightly simplified Holmes's compliment to the stature of his opponent: ". . . if I were assured of your destruction I would, in the interests of the public, cheerfully accept my own." Gillette links Moriarty to the Faulkner case and has the arch-villain scheme to trap Holmes in a sealed room and gas him to death.

A weakness of the stage piece is that Holmes is the master of every situation. There is no space for the effort, skill and patience that is emphasized in the stories. Holmes becomes more improbable than he should be. Watson has little to do, having been robbed of his role as narrator and commentator, and an important dimension of the original stories has been lost. There is no Mrs Hudson, and a page-boy called Billy, based on the boy Conan Doyle mentioned in *A Case of Identity*, shows in visitors. (Conan Doyle reintroduced the boy to later stories and took up the name Billy.) Moriarty fails in his schemes and is formidable only thanks to his past record and his powerful manner in threatening Holmes in their interview. Here his only accomplishment is to burn down 221B Baker Street (in *The Final Problem*, he merely started a small fire in Holmes's rooms), but Holmes has no further need of the place anyway. He plans a trip to the Continent, and Moriarty promises to follow: "I shall meet you there . . . and you know it. And when I fall, you will fall with me." A nice hint of the Reichenbach encounter!

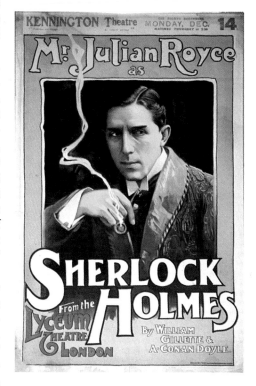

Julian Royce was one of the many lesser-known interpreters of Sherlock Holmes. He starred in a touring company from 1902 to 1904, and this poster refers to the presentation of Gillette's play at a South London theatre.

Many bits and pieces from other stories pleasantly surface, such as the way Holmes slips the handcuffs on Moriarty (taken from *A Study in Scarlet*), his indulgence in a seven-per-cent solution and his deduction based on the poorly-shaven right side of Watson's face (derived from *The Boscombe Valley Mystery*). And it is in this play that the celebrated phrase "Elementary, my dear Watson," has its origin, although in slightly longer form: "Oh, this is elementary, my dear Watson." Furthermore, it was Gillette who added a curved pipe to the Holmesian image. (Paget's illustrations had shown a straight one.)

William Gillette frequently revived the play on American tours and eventually played Holmes over 1,200 times. To American audiences, illustrators and later film-makers, he was for many years the definitive image of how Sherlock Holmes should look. As in Paget's work, it was a more handsome Holmes that Conan Doyle had originally described, and now he was a romantic idol as well! But Conan Doyle did not argue with success: "You make the poor hero of the anaemic printed page a very limp object as compared with the glamour of your own personality which you infuse into his stage presentment," he told Gillette. While Conan Doyle's stories had already stimulated a few theatrical burlesques, the Gillette play encouraged many more, including one by Gillette himself: the one-act *Painful Predicament of Sherlock Holmes*, in which a lady client talks so much that Holmes never gets a word in edgeways.

In July 1903, for the part of the page-boy in a touring production of the play, the 14-year-old Charlie Chaplin was selected. It was a great boost to his career, and it is interesting to connect him with Holmes for Chaplin's creation of the "gentleman tramp" in bowler hat and baggy trousers with the bent cane is the only character as universally recognizable in silhouette as the great detective.

THE RETURN OF SHERLOCK HOLMES

Shortly after William Gillette's play had opened in New York, Arthur Conan Doyle's full attention was taken up by the Boer War, which broke out in October 1899. He decided to write a full history of the conflict as it happened and spent several months on the ground in South Africa during 1900. His book *The Great Boer War* was published in October of that year.

In March 1901, Conan Doyle went on a golfing holiday at Cromer, Norfolk, with a friend called Fletcher Robinson who related to him the West Country legend of a spectral dog. This inspired the writing of the best-known of all the Sherlock Holmes stories, *The Hound of the Baskervilles*. The Devon-born Robinson showed Conan Doyle the Dartmoor area and helped provide local colour for the story. It was not originally intended to feature Sherlock Holmes, but the sleuth had soon worked his way in as a leading character. Conan Doyle did not go so far as to revive Holmes from his watery death in *The Final Problem*, but rather he made it a reminiscence by Watson of a case that had happened some time beforehand. The story was written for serialization in *The Strand Magazine*, and it appeared over nine months from August 1901 to April 1902, building up a huge following. Long queues of eager readers formed at publisher George Newnes's offices in Southampton Street when a new instalment was due off the presses.

The Hound of the Baskervilles is rightly regarded as the finest of the four Sherlock Holmes novels. Conan Doyle was a powerful writer of supernatural stories. (He had recently contributed to the *Strand* a story called *The Brown Hand* about a ghost in search of its amputated hand and he later wrote *The Terror of Blue John Gap*, which was about a beast living in Derbyshire caves, ten times the size of a bear with a red, gaping mouth, monstrous fangs and white, sightless eyes.) Here he makes vivid the legend of an enormous supernatural hound that plagues the family of Baskervilles (the long flashback to the legend's origin appears early in this story). Conan Doyle's gifts as a descriptive writer, which had conveyed the setting of the Reichenbach Falls so powerfully in *The Final Problem*, here keenly evoked the atmosphere of the moors and made the bleak setting a potent factor in the events he had Watson relate. Although Holmes soon guesses the identity of the villain – the clues to what is going on are fairly presented and there is a paucity of suspects – he is faced with an audacious and skilful adversary.

Holmes himself is not prominent for a long section of the story, and Watson carries out the preliminary investigations in Devon. It is the only occasion on which Holmes congratulates Watson on his detective work: the doctor even tracks down the mysterious man on the moors, who turns out to be Holmes himself, working on the case in his own way. Holmes had fooled Watson into thinking that he was still in Baker Street, and it seems another indication of his cold and mistrustful outlook that he did not take Watson into his confidence. In order to conclude the case satisfactorily and nab his man, Holmes lays a trap that proves nearly fatal to Sir Henry Baskerville who is unknowingly the bait and might have been safer had Holmes put him in the picture.

The story was cleverly written to keep *Strand* readers hooked. The first instalment had Doctor Mortimer relating to Sherlock Holmes and Watson the circumstances of Sir Charles Baskerville's death and mentioning footprints he alone observed near the body:

"Footprints?"

"Footprints."

"A man's or a woman's?"

Dr Mortimer looked strangely at us for an instant, and his voice sank almost to a whisper as he answered:–

"Mr Holmes, they were the footprints of a gigantic hound."

(To be continued)

And then there is Doctor Watson waiting for the man on the moors to return to his hiding place:

And then at last I heard him. Far away came the sharp clink of a boot striking upon a stone. Then another and yet another, coming nearer and nearer. I shrank back into the darkest corner and cocked the pistol in my pocket, determined not to discover myself until I had an opportunity of seeing something of the stranger. There was a long pause which showed that he had stopped. Then once more the footsteps approached and a shadow fell across the opening of the hut.

"It is a lovely evening, my dear Watson," said a well-known voice. "I really think that you will be more comfortable outside than in."

(To be continued)

Above left, Sherlock Holmes and Watson exchange glances with the man in the hansom cab who is following their client, Sir Henry Baskerville, down Regent Street in *The Hound of the Baskervilles*. This is Sidney Paget's illustration as it appeared in the *Strand*, and it is sometimes claimed that it was printed in reverse – however, Regent Street is shown curving in the proper direction, and the traffic is moving along the correct side of the road. Sidney Paget illustrated the chapter ending in which Watson sees the shadow fall across the entrance to the place where the mysterious man of the moors is living.

Above left, Sidney Paget's illustrations for the *Strand* serialization of *The Hound of the Baskervilles* included the dramatic moment when Holmes empties five barrels of his revolver into the hound's flanks as it attacks Sir Henry. Above right, the foremost American illustrator of the Holmes stories, Frederic Dorr Steele, worked on this story in connection with the release of Hollywood's 1939 film starring Basil Rathbone. This is one of four drawings he made showing Holmes on Dartmoor.

Opposite, the first Holmes story that Frederic Dorr Steele illustrated was *The Adventure of the Empty House*. For the cover of *Collier's* in which it appeared, he provided this striking study of Holmes at the Reichenbach Falls following Moriarty's plunge into the abyss.

It must be, it can only be, Sherlock Holmes – but imagine having to wait a whole month to find out more!

Before this instalment came out, however, one reader had published a complaint about the story. Frank Sidgwick addressed an open letter to Dr Watson in the *Cambridge Review* in which he pointed out a number of inconsistencies. For example, the story is clearly dated as occurring in 1889 and Watson is living at Baker Street with Holmes, yet in *The Sign of Four* the good doctor had become engaged to Mary Morstan in September 1888 and married her "a few months later". It was the first example of Sherlockian criticism.

An avid reader of the Holmes adventures was King Edward VII, who had become friendly with Conan Doyle. When stories circulated of British atrocities during the Boer War, Conan Doyle wrote a pamphlet that rebutted the charges, *The War in South Africa – Its Cause and Conduct*. For his services on behalf of his country's reputation, he was knighted at Buckingham Palace on 9 August 1902. It was during this month too that a second series of stories about his historical character Brigadier Gerard began appearing in *The Strand Magazine* over eight issues; they were published in novel form as *Adventures of Gerard* in 1903.

When *Collier's*, the weekly magazine in New York, offered Sir Arthur a record sum to write from five to thirteen new stories that would resurrect Sherlock Holmes from his watery grave, he succumbed, only to find it difficult to devise enough

IN THIS NUMBER —"THE RETURN OF SHERLOCK HOLMES"

Beginning a New Series of Detective Stories by A. CONAN DOYLE

Collier's

Household Number for October

DRAWN BY FREDERIC DORR STEELE

VOL XXXI NO 26   SEPTEMBER 26 1903   PRICE 10 CENTS

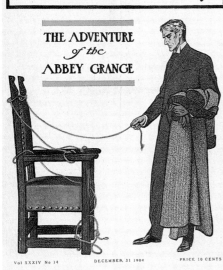

Four more of Frederic Dorr Steele's covers for *Collier's*, showing the issues that brought to American readers *The Adventure of the Golden Pince-Nez* (above left), *The Adventure of the Abbey Grange* (below left), *The Adventure of the Solitary Cyclist* (left), and *A Reminiscence of Mr Sherlock Holmes*, later known as *The Adventure of Wisteria Lodge* (above).

interesting and unrepetitive plots. He managed to provide 13 new adventures, but he always liked to quote a Cornish fisherman who told him that Sherlock Holmes was "never quite the same man afterwards" (after the Reichenbach Falls incident), as it justified his doubts over reviving the sleuth. Certainly the new Sherlock Holmes was a changed man – not quite so eccentric or surprising as before, and no longer using cocaine (or at least Watson never mentions it; although it was still not illegal, its use was becoming frowned upon).

The new stories were taken by *The Strand Magazine* for British publication, and Sidney Paget again illustrated them. But *Collier's* engaged Frederic Dorr Steele, who provided 11 impressive colour covers as well as other drawings inside. Steele depicted Sherlock Holmes quite differently from Paget. He modelled Holmes on William Gillette, working at least once from a stage photograph and so helping to perpetuate this image of Holmes. But Steele's representation was closer to Conan Doyle's idea of the man – more hawkfaced and approaching more to the Red Indian type.

In the first of the new stories, *The Adventure of the Empty House*, Conan Doyle tackled the problem of bringing Sherlock Holmes back to life. The detective, unable as always to resist a touch of the theatrical, fools Watson completely with his disguise as an elderly bookseller, causing his biographer to faint when he realizes that it is Holmes, alive and well! Holmes's reason for staying away for three years and not letting Watson know of his survival is unconvincing, as is the extraordinary outline of his travels during which, among other highlights, he became a famous Norwegian explorer called Sigerson. But no one minded, as long as Sherlock Holmes was back in action! Moriarty is dead but Holmes fools his henchman, Colonel Sebastian Moran, into taking a shot at a wax bust positioned in the window of 221B Baker Street.

At the beginning of *The Adventure of the Norwood Builder*, a bored Holmes laments the passing of Moriarty, "the great malignant brain" whose activities made life such a challenge. But when the unhappy John Hector McFarlane bursts in a few steps ahead of arrest by police, Holmes perks up immediately and almost commits a

verbal gaffe when he remarks, "This is really most grati – most interesting". Holmes clears McFarlane and shows up the insolent, cocksure Inspector Lestrade once again. As in *A Scandal in Bohemia*, he stages a fire alarm in order to startle someone into giving himself away.

In *The Adventure of the Dancing Men*, Holmes solves the mystery of the coded messages in the form of cavorting stick figures that are frightening the wife of Norfolk squire Hilton Cubitt. The code clearly owes its inspiration to the cipher in Poe's *The Gold-Bug*. Conan Doyle creates another area of Holmesian expertise as the detective declares: "I am fairly familiar with all forms of secret writings, and am myself the author of a trifling monograph upon the subject, in which I analyse one hundred and sixty separate ciphers." But it is one of the darker cases in the canon: Holmes's client is killed and the detective has to be content with capturing the villain, a Chicago gangster called Abe Slaney.

Miss Violet Smith, a private tutor in music from Farnham in Surrey, brings Sherlock Holmes *The Adventure of the Solitary Cyclist*. Our sleuth, too busy on other cases to investigate the lone rider who shadows Miss Smith on her trips across a lonely stretch of countryside, dispatches Watson to investigate. This time it is not a ruse to fool Watson as in *The Hound of the Baskervilles*, the overlap of cases giving a more convincing picture of life at 221B. But Holmes had to participate in the case –

In contrast to *Collier's*, *The Strand Magazine* always retained its basic cover design with modifications. The September 1914 cover (left) included Frank Wiles's full-colour illustration for *The Valley of Fear*, reproduced at full page size inside (and reproduced later in this book on page 56). The January 1927 cover (centre) introduced some seasonal snow to the street scene behind a transparent head of Holmes – this issue contained one of the very last stories, *The Adventure of the Retired Colourman*. The January 1924 issue (above) contained *The Adventure of the Sussex Vampire*. These covers are among the rare items photographed from the Stanley MacKenzie Collection for this book.

An illustration by Frederic Dorr Steele for *Collier's* showing the capture of Abe Slaney in *The Adventure of the Dancing Men*, published in the 5 December 1903 issue. Holmes, the local police inspector and Watson confront the villain. Below, watched by Watson, Holmes claps Inspector Lestrade on the shoulder in *The Adventure of the Norwood Builder*. Holmes has not only saved Lestrade from making a fool of himself but now offers him the glory for having solved the case. This illustration by Sidney Paget appeared in the November 1903 *Strand*.

the editor of *The Strand Magazine* rejected the original draft, insisting that Holmes be given more to do – and so Watson's work is declared shoddy ("You have done remarkably badly"), and Holmes himself takes up the scent. A thrilling climax finds him too late to prevent a forced marriage in the woods but in time to apprehend the villains and to point out that the ceremony has no legal validity. This is one of the occasions when Watson neglects to help an injured man in order to stay in the chase.

It is to the Peak District that Holmes and Watson travel in *The Adventure of the Priory School* to solve the kidnapping of the 10-year-old son of the Duke of Holdernesse from his private school. The story has some weak points. Not only is the reader asked to believe that a constable was watching a lonely crossroads all night for no given reason and that another road was under continuous surveillance pending the arrival of a doctor, but Holmes, demonstrating another field of expertise, reads the direction a bicycle has travelled from its tracks. When readers protested that it was impossible, Conan Doyle carried out some tests and said he was right, but in later years he did admit that he had made a mistake. Only the direction of splash marks from water or mud would indicate which way a bicycle had gone.

Holmes is given an enormous fee of £6,000 by the Duke for his work, and Watson not only remarks on "an appearance of avidity which was a surprise to me, who knew his frugal tastes" but also concludes the story strangely:

> Holmes folded up his cheque, and placed it carefully in his notebook. "I am a poor man," said he, as he patted it affectionately, and thrust it into the depths of his inner pocket.

In the following month's story, *The Adventure of Black Peter*, Conan Doyle evidently had second thoughts about the curious impression his previous ending had given and has Watson declare:

> Holmes . . . like all great artists, lived for his art's sake, and save in the case of the Duke of Holdernesse, I have seldom known him claim any large reward for his inestimable services. So unworldly was he – or so capricious – that he frequently refused his help to the powerful and wealthy where the problem made no appeal to his sympathies, while he would devote weeks of most intense application to the affairs of some humble client whose case presented those strange and dramatic qualities which appealed to his imagination and challenged his ingenuity.

In this story, former whaler captain Peter Carey is found harpooned to death in his outhouse in Essex, and Inspector Stanley Hopkins prevails on Holmes to take a look at the case. Holmes lures the murderer to his Baker Street quarters and snaps the handcuffs on him as he had on the killer in *A Study in Scarlet*.

The detective shows his practical side in *The Adventure of Charles Augustus Milverton* when, on behalf of a woman client, he attempts to purchase some imprudent letters from Milverton, the king of blackmailers. The repulsive Milverton, with his "plump, hairless face", sets an impossibly high price, and Holmes attempts to wrest the papers from him. The detective then takes the law into his own hands by burgling Milverton's safe and burning the contents. (Holmes seems to be taking a leaf from the book of Raffles, the amateur cracksman invented by Conan Doyle's brother-in-law, E. W. Hornung.) He and Watson chance to witness one of Milverton's victims, shoot him dead and grind her heel in his upturned face. The pair are spotted hastening from the scene (but not recognized), and we obtain the only full description of Watson – "a middle-sized, strongly built man – square jaw, thick neck, moustache . . ." – when Inspector Lestrade visits Baker Street and requests Holmes's help in catching the fleeing murderers! Holmes tells Lestrade: "I think there are certain crimes which the law cannot touch, and which, therefore, to some extent, justify private revenge . . . My sympathies are with the criminals rather than with the victim, and I will not handle the case."

This Number Contains Sherlock Holmes' Sixth Adventure

Collier's

Household Number for March

Two more of Frederic Dorr Steele's memorable covers for *Collier's*. The issue below carried the first American publication of *The Adventure of the Norwood Builder*, and Steele has taken the liberty of enlarging a bloody thumb print into an entire hand. The issue, dated 27 February 1904 (right), presented *The Adventure of Black Peter* to American readers.

VOL XXXII NO 22   FEBRUARY 27 1904   PRICE 10 CENTS

Collier's

Household Number for November

Sherlock Holmes

In this Number Solves
The Mystery of

The
Norwood Builder

PRICE 10 CENTS

OCTOBER 31 1903

VOL XXXII NO 5

When *Collier's* published *The Adventure of the Six Napoleons* in its 30 April 1904 issue, Frederic Dorr Steele provided this illustration of Holmes striking a bust of Napoleon with his hunting crop.

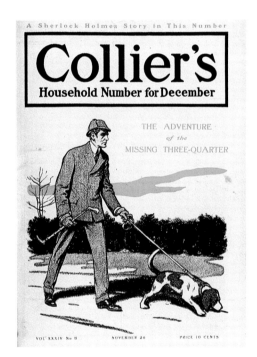

The draghound Pompey leads the way as Sherlock Holmes looks for the vanished rugger player in *The Adventure of the Missing Three-Quarter*. A Steele cover for *Collier's*, 26 November 1904.

In *The Adventure of the Six Napoleons*, Holmes helps Lestrade solve the mystery of identical plaster statues of Napoleon that are being stolen and smashed. The explanation is obvious (and recalls *The Blue Carbuncle*), but Holmes plays a close hand as usual and brings matters to a theatrical climax when he smashes the last of six busts and recovers a missing pearl. Watson writes:

Lestrade and I sat silent for a moment, and then, with a spontaneous impulse, we both broke out clapping, as at the well-wrought climax of a play. A flush of colour sprang to Holmes's pale cheeks, and he bowed to us like the master dramatist who receives the homage of his audience. It was at such moments that for an instant he ceased to be a reasoning machine, and betrayed his human love for admiration and applause.

Holmes buys the last bust from the owner without revealing its contents; he pays a generous price but clearly has no intention of sharing the reward, although Doctor Watson doesn't go into details.

While researching into early English charters at "one of our great university towns" in *The Adventure of the Three Students*, the great detective is persuaded to pinpoint which of three students has copied an examination paper in advance. The most obvious suspect is the guilty one, and scandal is avoided. The story does not earn high marks.

In *The Adventure of the Golden Pince-Nez*, Holmes dazzles Inspector Hopkins with the information he gleans from studying a pince-nez. It has been found in the hands of a murdered male secretary who worked for a professor in the Kent countryside. As in earlier stories, a murky history of betrayal in a distant land is at the bottom of the affair.

The key player in the Cambridge rugger team disappears on the night before the big match in *The Adventure of the Missing Three-Quarter*. Holmes's efforts to locate the missing man are strongly resisted by a certain Dr Leslie Armstrong. The case is interesting because Holmes mistakes Armstrong for a villain: "I have not seen a man who, if he turns his talents that way, was more calculated to fill the gap left by the illustrious Moriarty." In fact, Dr Armstrong is simply doing his best to prevent scandal and he makes a valid criticism of Holmes's line of work: "Where your calling is more open to criticism is when you pry into the secrets of private individuals, when you rake up family matters which are better hidden, and when you incidentally waste the time of men who are more busy than yourself." Holmes's persistence amounts, in Armstrong's words, to "monstrous conduct" and there is nothing for the detective to do at the end but quietly withdraw from a scene of domestic tragedy and promise his discretion. The conclusion recalls that of *The Yellow Face*.

One of the best openings of any case begins *The Adventure of the Abbey Grange*:

> It was on a bitterly cold and frosty morning during the winter of '97 that I was wakened by a tugging at my shoulder. It was Holmes. The candle in his hand shone upon his eager, stooping face, and told me at a glance that something was amiss.
>
> "Come, Watson, come!" he cried. "The game is afoot. Not a word! Into your clothes and come!"

This is the only time that Holmes is quoted as saying "The game is afoot" (the expression used by the King in Shakespeare's *Henry V*), although Watson writes the same words in narrating the later *Adventure of Wisteria Lodge*.

The investigation, which concerns the violent death of the detestable Sir Eustace Brackenstall, is notable because Holmes is nearly deceived by a faked burglary. This is also one of the best instances of Holmes taking the law into his own hands and acquitting the killer: "So long as the law does not find some other victim you are

Holmes, in his country deerstalker, followed by Watson, discovers the body of a German teacher on the moor in the Peak District during *The Adventure of the Priory School*. Sidney Paget's illustration appeared in the *Strand* dated February 1904.

The opening page from the *Strand*'s publication of *The Adventure of the Abbey Grange* when, once again, "the game is afoot". Sidney Paget shows the eager Holmes awakening his companion.

safe from me." Holmes even mocks the legal system (by which, he says in another story, "many men have been wrongfully hanged"), staging a quick trial with himself as judge and Watson as the jury.

Conan Doyle made a new attempt to finish with Sherlock Holmes when he supplied *Collier's* with the thirteenth and final commissioned story. *The Adventure of the Second Stain* was announced as "The Last Sherlock Holmes Story Ever To Be Written", and *Collier's* had arranged with E. W. Hornung to follow on with new Raffles stories. Watson informs us that Sherlock Holmes is no longer interested in having his old work publicized now that he has retired to study and keep bees on the Sussex Downs. But the doctor has gained special permission to relate "the most important international case which he has ever been called upon to handle". The Prime Minister personally seeks Holmes's assistance in recovering a document that could start a war. In clearing up the case, the sleuth is surprisingly kind towards a politician's wife who has jeopardized both the peace and her husband's career, and there is a delightful moment of understanding at the very end between Holmes and the shrewd Prime Minister over the former's diplomatic handling of the matter.

At the same time as the story appeared, Americans were playing a new card game called *Sherlock Holmes*, launched for Christmas 1904 by Parker Bros. Around this period, too, there was the first serious film adaptation of Conan Doyle's work, made by the Vitagraph Company, which had been established in New York by two Englishmen. One of them, J. Stuart Blackton, directed the 12-minute-long *The Adventures of Sherlock Holmes*, based on *The Sign of Four* and starring a well-known stage actor, Maurice Costello, as the Baker Street detective. This had been preceded by *Sherlock Holmes Baffled*, a 30-second film in which the detective is outwitted by a burglar who, thanks to trick photography, keeps disappearing and reappearing.

6 HIS LAST BOW?

George Edalji was one of the real-life victims of injustice for whom Arthur Conan Doyle battled in the manner of Sherlock Holmes.

Sir Arthur Conan Doyle was now free to research and write another painstaking but ponderous set of medieval stories, serialized in *The Strand Magazine* from December 1905 to December 1906 and illustrated by Arthur Twidle. They were issued in book form as *Sir Nigel*. In 1906 Conan Doyle had a mild success with a New York stage production, *Brigadier Gerard*, based on his stories, but the death of his wife Louise in July was a great blow. At the end of the year, he became interested in the case of George Edalji, a myopic Parsee and junior barrister who had been convicted of maiming animals. Scotland Yard permitted Conan Doyle to examine the evidence, and he wrote a series of articles for *The Daily Telegraph* early in 1907. He made it obvious that Edalji was innocent, but, although the man was released from jail, he was never officially cleared. It was an instance of Conan Doyle himself donning the mantle (or cape) of Sherlock Holmes, but he refused most requests to investigate actual cases.

In 1907 he re-married – his new wife was an old friend, Jean Leckie – and in 1908 he gave in yet again and wrote two further Sherlock Holmes stories. He provided *Collier's* and *The Strand Magazine* with what is now known as *The Adventure of Wisteria Lodge*, although it then had the title of *A Reminiscence of Mr Sherlock Holmes* and the spelling was Wistaria in the magazines. Sidney Paget had died earlier in the year, and Arthur Twidle capably illustrated the story in England, while Frederic Dorr Steele was again commissioned by *Collier's*. The *Strand* ran the story in two parts.

Singular as the experience of Mr Scott Eccles has been as a guest at Wistaria Lodge, it seems improbable that he would be so concerned by the disappearance of his host as to seek out Sherlock Holmes's assistance before it is known that murder is involved. Holmes makes an unusually early disclosure of his conclusions so that the first part of the story becomes more satisfying. The second half bogs down in an account of South American politics and has an anti-climax when the villains flee before Holmes and the police can deal with them. The adventure features the brightest of all the police inspectors to figure in the canon, a man called Baynes, who independently follows the same trail as Holmes and even observes the master detective crawling about in shrubbery without being noticed himself. It is to Holmes's credit that he is as unstinting in his praise of Baynes as he is in his condemnation of Lestrade and others.

The second story, *The Adventure of the Bruce-Partington Plans*, reintroduces Sherlock's brother Mycroft who is now revealed as "the most indispensable man in the country". ("Occasionally he *is* the British government," Holmes informs Watson.) Mycroft asks his brother to recover some missing submarine plans; this Holmes does by brilliant deductions and by becoming a burglar, allowing Lestrade to comment, "No wonder you get results that are beyond us." Holmes also gets an emerald tie-pin from Queen Victoria as a reward for his efforts although he refuses a place in the next honours list.

A series of Sherlock Holmes short films made by Nordisk of Copenhagen began appearing. Surviving examples (like *The Confidence Trick*) show that only the name was borrowed. The short, stocky Holmes in a huge cloth cap doesn't even have a Watson, and the crude capers are a thousand miles from Baker Street. The Gillette play had become a huge hit in France, where the translator had added a further

Believe it or not, that's Sherlock Holmes, Danish-style, with his ear to the wall in one of a series of crude silent film adventures. This is *Droske 519 (Cab No. 519)*, released in 1909, with Viggo Larsen as the sleuth.

Oscar Slater was another recipient of Conan Doyle's efforts to correct injustice, but their relationship was far from cordial.

scene (based on *The Empty House*) in which Moriarty shoots a dummy of Holmes set up in a window. French author Maurice Leblanc had planned that his gentleman burglar, Arsène Lupin, should meet Sherlock Holmes in his latest novel, but he was stopped by Conan Doyle, and the book was retitled *Arsène Lupin contre Herlock Sholmes*, Watson becoming Wilson. (A German film version ignored the change and was released as *Arsène Lupin Against Sherlock Holmes*.)

In 1909 Sir Arthur became interested in two real-life causes. He campaigned against slavery in the Belgian Congo, and he took up the cause of an unsavoury figure called Oscar Slater, who had been convicted, on flimsy evidence, of killing an elderly spinster. Slater was not pardoned until 1928 when Conan Doyle helped pay the legal fees for an inquiry.

The stage renewed its appeal to Conan Doyle, who leased London theatres and financed productions of *The Fires of Fate* (from his story *The Tragedy of the Korosko*) and *The House of Temperley* (from his boxing drama *Rodney Stone*). He followed this with a three-act adaptation of his Sherlock Holmes story, *The Speckled Band*. Although this was poorly structured (Holmes makes a very belated appearance), it had a huge success. Conan Doyle engaged H. A. Saintsbury to be his sleuth (the actor had starred in a company touring with the Gillette play), while Lyn Harding played the evil Grimesby Rylott (as he is renamed) and made the biggest impression.

In 1910 *The Strand Magazine* published another Sherlock Holmes story, *The Adventure of the Devil's Foot*, with a new illustrator Gilbert Holiday, whose work was uninspired. In this story, as in *The Reigate Squire*, Watson takes Holmes on holiday to recover from exhaustion, but a case inevitably arises. Holmes suspects that poisonous fumes may have been responsible for a woman's death and the brain damage to her two brothers. He involves Watson in conducting a test that nearly claims their lives – Watson is delighted at the chance to save Holmes instead of being upset by the narrowness of his escape! Despite the close shave, Holmes again acts as judge and jury and finds sufficient mitigating circumstances to permit the murderer to leave the country.

In 1911 two further cases appeared in the *Strand* with new and barely adequate illustrators. *The Adventure of the Red Circle* was a two-part case in which Holmes's investigation into a landlady's mysterious lodger intersects with the work of Scotland Yard and the American Pinkerton Agency. There is little for any of the detectives to do as the notorious leader of the New York Italian criminal brotherhood, called the Red Circle, meets his just deserts from the former gang member he is pursuing.

In *The Disappearance of Lady Frances Carfax*, Doctor Watson is dispatched to Lausanne by Holmes to look for the missing lady. As in *The Hound of the Baskervilles*, Holmes also takes a hand without informing Watson and, disguised as a French workman, makes a dramatic appearance on the scene. This time Watson receives no praise for his efforts. Instead he is castigated by Holmes: "I cannot at the moment recall any possible blunder which you have omitted." Watson is momentarily bitter, but as always forgives. Holmes himself is slow to realize the fairly obvious significance of an over-size coffin, and Watson has his uses, reviving Lady Frances after she is rescued from burial alive in the nick of time. The despicable Holy Peters is a memorable addition to the canon's gallery of rogues.

During the same year, Conan Doyle wrote *The Lost World*, probably his most famous book apart from the Holmes stories. For this adventure story he created a new hero, Professor George E. Challenger, whom he hoped would challenge Holmes's popularity. The story was serialized in *The Strand Magazine* in 1912. Also published this year was the booklet *The Case of Oscar Slater*, which led to a first, inconclusive inquiry into the affair. A new series of properly licensed screen

H. A. Saintsbury was a distinguished impersonator of Conan Doyle's great detective on stage and screen, here shown as he appeared in the play *The Speckled Band* in 1910.

Not for the only time, Sherlock Holmes has taken a risk. His experiment with a suspected poisonous substance in *The Adventure of the Devil's Foot* almost costs him and Watson their lives. The good doctor manages to rescue himself and Holmes and readily forgives his friend. They are shown recovering in the open air in Gilbert Holiday's illustration from the *Strand*, December 1910.

The *Strand*'s December 1911 issue contained *The Disappearance of Lady Frances Carfax*.

An illustration by Alec Ball shows the disguised Holmes coming to Watson's rescue in a French street. *The Disappearance of Lady Frances Carfax* was the only story illustrated by Ball.

adaptations of eight of the Sherlock Holmes short stories went into production in England during the year, with French actor Georges Treville as the detective (he only had to look and act the part, of course; his speech didn't matter in silent films).

The year 1912 was further notable for a paper delivered by Ronald A. Knox (later a prominent Roman Catholic bishop) to the Gryphon Society at Trinity College, Oxford, which was later published. Called *Studies in the Literature of Sherlock Holmes*, it was a witty, mock-scholarly piece, which examined the basic structure of the stories and the order in which they had occurred according to the internal evidence of dating, and mentioned some of the inconsistencies and implausibilities. Knox also raised the eternally intriguing issue of whether Sherlock Holmes was an Oxford or Cambridge man.

Late in 1913, *Collier's* and the *Strand* published a new memoir, *The Adventure of the Dying Detective*. *Collier's* used Frederic Dorr Steele once again, while the *Strand* belatedly gave Walter Paget the opportunity to illustrate a Sherlock Holmes story. The great detective has fasted for three days and applied make-up to convince Mrs Hudson and Watson that he is at death's door so that he can trap a murderer; he explains to Watson that he had to be fooled to play his part properly, but the doctor is too relieved to find Holmes fit and well to make any complaint. This was the only story Walter Paget illustrated and, as Holmes was not supposed to be looking his usual self, it is difficult to comment on whether he would have been a better artist than his late brother.

It was the illustrator of the next Holmes story who earned Conan Doyle's highest

praise. This was Frank Wiles, and the story was the novel-length *The Valley of Fear*, first serialized in *The Strand Magazine* from September 1914 to May 1915. Wiles provided a splendid colour frontispiece of Holmes examining a coded message he has received from one of Moriarty's henchmen. "This comes nearest to my conception of what Holmes really looks like," said Sir Arthur.

Like *A Study in Scarlet* and *The Sign of Four*, *The Valley of Fear* has a long explanatory flashback without Holmes; in fact, past events take up more space than the modern story. Holmes investigates a death at a manor house in Sussex; he alone works out the significance of the single dumb-bell and produces the principal missing witness (echoing the climax of *The Norwood Builder*). Moriarty is never seen or heard and the police are not convinced that he is the evil controlling genius painted by Holmes. He has undertaken to kill the American detective who infiltrated a criminal brotherhood in a mining community in the United States and brought its leaders to justice. (Conan Doyle based his story on the actual events that had taken place in Pennsylvania, when the Molly Maguires had been broken up by a Pinkerton agent.) Though Moriarty is outwitted for the moment, there is a sting at the end of the tale when his eventual success is noted, leaving Sherlock Holmes to exclaim, "I don't say he can't be beat. But you must give me time – you must give me time!" before lapsing into thoughtful silence. This is the only case reported by Watson in which Moriarty is involved before his actual appearance in *The Final Problem*.

The year 1914 was also significant for the appearance of two rival screen versions

How two artists depicted the great detective feigning a deadly illness in *The Adventure of the Dying Detective*. Walter Paget in the *Strand* (opposite) shows Holmes deserting his bed to lock the door and prevent Watson from leaving to bring help. For *Collier's*, Frederic Dorr Steele provided this impression (above) of the gaunt, wasted-looking Holmes who chilled Watson's heart with his stare.

of the first Sherlock Holmes story. The British *A Study in Scarlet* was a full-length, properly licensed adaptation by the Samuelson company, which opened with the Mormon sequence and only introduced Holmes late in the picture. He was played by James Bragington, an employee of the production company's Birmingham branch office who had never acted before but who was cast on the basis of his gaunt appearance. He certainly looked the part to judge from the surviving photographs. The American *A Study in Scarlet* was unauthorized. The two-reel production was made by Universal, with Francis Ford (brother of John) both starring as Holmes and directing from a script by his wife Grace Cunard.

A feature-length German version of *The Hound of the Baskervilles* was also

Artist Frank Wiles was responsible for this excellent full-colour study of Holmes which faced the start of serialization of *The Valley of Fear* in the *Strand*'s issue for September 1914. It shows Holmes pondering over the message in cipher he has received from an informant.

released in 1914 just before the outbreak of World War One. Its sets should have been impressive, since they were designed by Hermann Warm, the Expressionist who later worked on *The Cabinet of Dr Caligari*, and in general it seems to have been the first screen work based on a Holmes story to involve major talents. Several other German films featuring Holmes were made during this wartime period, but they had little or nothing to do with Conan Doyle.

In 1916 the Samuelson company released a second Holmes adaptation, *The Valley of Fear*, based on the most recent story. This time H. A. Saintsbury, who had by now played Sherlock Holmes on stage over 1,000 times (in both the Gillette play and Conan Doyle's own production of *The Speckled Band*) took the key role, and, as in

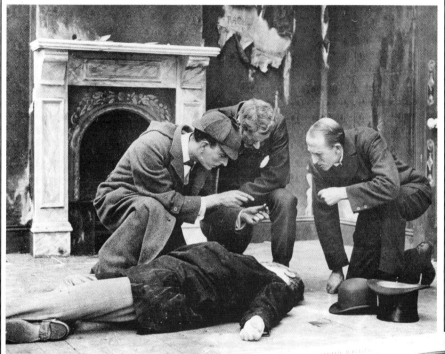

Sherlock Holmes (James Bragington) has discovered a woman's wedding ring beside the corpse of Enoch J. Drebber in the 1914 British film version of *A Study in Scarlet*. Watson and Lestrade study the find. The word RACHE may again be seen behind them where the wallpaper has been torn off.

Holmes at work in *The Valley of Fear*, drawn by Frank Wiles for the *Strand*'s serialization. He is seen examining the body at Birlstone Manor.

A classic scene from the 1916 film of Gillette's play, *Sherlock Holmes*: William Gillette's Sherlock Holmes is taking no chances with Moriarty (Ernest Maupain) when the latter visits Baker Street to meet the thorn in his side. The pageboy Billy (Burford Hampden) helps his master deal with the Napoleon of Crime.

Holmes as scientific experimenter, posed by William Gillette for the film *Sherlock Holmes*. This is seemingly the only film in which the celebrated actor ever appeared.

Sir Arthur Conan Doyle, c. 1916.

later adaptations of the story, Moriarty (played by Booth Conway) was directly involved in the action.

The same year saw the appearance of an American film version of William Gillette's stage play. It was filmed in Chicago by the Essanay company and starred Gillette himself. The original play was opened out and the romantic element further emphasized: Holmes's eye is taken by the beauty of Alice Faulkner on a chance encounter even before he is engaged to recover the papers from her. It is regrettable that these film records of Gillette and Saintsbury, the two foremost stage portrayers of Sherlock Holmes, do not seem to have survived. Orson Welles remembered Gillette from his stage work as "the inventor of underplaying", and it would be valuable to see if he avoided the over-emphasis of much silent screen acting.

For Conan Doyle, 1916 was important as the year in which he became convinced of life after death, and his major concern from then on was to try to spread belief in spiritualism. He became its foremost supporter, and his books, lectures and interviews on the subject made him the butt of some ridicule, but his sincerity was never in question.

When a French general raised the question of how Sherlock Holmes might have contributed to the war effort, Conan Doyle was inspired to write *His Last Bow*. The story is set in August 1914 and Holmes is described as being 60, the most precise indication of his age in any of the stories. The Prime Minister has personally called on him (he is still retired on the South Downs) to request that he break a German spy ring. The narrative tells of the culmination of two years' work in which Holmes has masqueraded as an Anglophobic Irish-American called Altamont (the middle name of Conan Doyle's father) and gained the Germans' confidence in Chicago (his work is reminiscent of the task accomplished by the detective in the flashback in *The Valley of Fear*).

This case is the first and only one to be related by an anonymous narrator; it is not told by Dr Watson. This is required by the structure of the story in which the master spy Von Bork is shown basking in his accomplishments at his base near Harwich

A. Gilbert illustrates the moment in *His Last Bow* when Holmes drops his masquerade as the German agent Altamont and chloroforms the master spy Von Bork. From the *Strand*, September 1917.

and awaiting the arrival of Altamont. Although it is no surprise when his visitor is revealed as Sherlock Holmes, the moment is deliciously handled as Von Bork discovers that instead of the British naval signals (which would allow England to be attacked within a week) he has been handed a copy of the *Practical Handbook of Bee Culture*:

> Only for one instant did the master spy glare at this strangely irrelevant inscription. The next he was gripped at the back of his neck by a grasp of iron, and a chloroformed sponge was held in front of his writhing face.

Holmes has summoned Doctor Watson in his automobile to participate in the climax. It is the only use of a motor car by Holmes that is recorded in the canon, where change is generally resisted, with little use even of the telephone.

The final page of Sir Arthur Conan Doyle's manuscript for *His Last Bow*, intended to be the ultimate word on Sherlock Holmes.

Furthermore, Holmes masquerades as a motor expert in this case. He has shown once again little regard for his old friend Watson, who has heard only indirectly that Holmes had retired to a farm on the South Downs. But there is warmth in their reunion – and a keen sense of fleeting time as Holmes says to Watson, "Stand with me here upon the terrace, for it may be the last quiet talk that we shall ever have", and they recall old times.

It is a splendid story, marred only by the very last sentence in which Holmes refers to his monetary gain from the case. Before that, there is his stirring speech about the war ahead.

> "There's an east wind coming, Watson."
> "I think not, Holmes. It is very warm."
> "Good old Watson! You are the one fixed point in a changing age. There's an east wind coming all the same, such a wind as never blew on England yet. It will be cold and bitter, Watson, and a good many of us may wither before its blast. But it's God's own wind none the less, and a cleaner, better, stronger land will lie in the sunshine when the storm has cleared."

Here at last seemed to be Sir Arthur's final story about Sherlock Holmes. There were now enough uncollected short stories to make up a volume for book publication in 1917, called *His Last Bow*. *The Adventure of the Cardboard Box* was included to help make up numbers and because the passage of time had removed the objections that had kept it from being anthologized earlier.

FURTHER FILMS AND FINAL CASES

Perhaps the oddest of all Holmesian screen interpretations dates from 1918, when an American company called Ebony Pictures made *Black Sherlock Holmes* with Sam Robinson in the title role, the only occasion the detective has been portrayed by a black actor.

In 1920 Conan Doyle sold to the British Stoll company the film rights to almost all the stories. Stoll embarked on 15 films known collectively as *The Adventures of Sherlock Holmes*, each around thirty minutes long. They were released as a group in April 1921 to be used as regular supporting material by cinemas. Stoll also made a feature-length version of *The Hound of the Baskervilles*, which was released in August 1921. All the Stoll films were directed by Maurice Elvey, who chose the 59-year-old Eille Norwood to portray Holmes and the even older-looking Hubert

Eille Norwood (1862–1948). He played the Sage of Baker Street in 47 silent films.

Willis to appear as Watson.★ Norwood was a stage star who had worked occasionally in films, and he had just made a strong impression starring in *The Tavern Knight* for Stoll. Willis was a busy screen and stage actor who had appeared in Conan Doyle's boxing play, *The House of Temperley*, back in 1910.

Sir Arthur was most impressed by Eille Norwood's performance, especially in his disguises, and he gave the actor the loud-patterned dressing-gown he wore for the Baker Street scenes. His only regret was that the action in the films had been moved to contemporary times. But, although Conan Doyle described the films as "quite wonderful" and although they were probably a vast improvement on the 1912 series, the shorts were considered dire by the film trade.

The *Kine Weekly* quite rightly referred to the practical impossibility of putting more than the dry bones of the stories on the screen. It was not just the short length but the lack of sound that made it impossible to convey the real flavour of the stories. Hubert Willis was thought to be totally miscast. His Watson is by far the dreariest and least essential of all the screen's doctors – mostly reduced to a blank who tags along behind Holmes. But Eille Norwood does make an impressive Holmes, bushy eye-browed, tall and authoritative, listening intently to clients, pressing his fingertips together, puffing on his pipe thoughtfully. He had clearly studied the stories, and it is easy to see why he earned Conan Doyle's respect. Yet he was badly let down by the scripts.

Two scenes from the 1921 film version of *A Scandal in Bohemia* in the series *The Adventures of Sherlock Holmes*. A heavily disguised Sherlock Holmes (Eille Norwood) pays a visit to Irene Adler (Joan Beverley), and Holmes at the conclusion of the case refuses the offer of a ring from his client, the King of Bohemia (Alfred Drayton), requesting instead the photograph of Irene Adler that he is holding. Doctor Watson (Hubert Willis) stands behind the two men.

★ In this same period, a young actor made his screen debut in two Stoll features directed by Elvey, *Innocent* and *The Fruitful Vine*. His name – Basil Rathbone. Almost thirty, he would have been ideal casting for Holmes in his prime.

In *The Dying Detective*, he writes down the most basic observations for the audience's benefit. His disguise fails to fool the villain, who strips it off him; and when this same adversary comes to Baker Street, he quickly spots the trap that has been laid for him (thanks to Watson's top hat, left conspicuously on view before the doctor goes into hiding). The police catch the man, not Holmes. It is all very ponderous, and the few beads of sweat on Norwood's brow hardly suggest the fasting that Holmes endured in the original story.

In *The Devil's Foot*, Holmes is on his rest cure but stumbles directly on to a case just seconds after Watson has said, "Thank goodness there won't be any work for you here!" This film errs in having Holmes rescue Watson (rather than the other way around) from the experiment with the poisonous fumes that goes wrong, and the box containing the deadly root bears a ludicrously enormous descriptive label.

In *A Case of Identity*, Mrs Hudson is amused and Dr Watson is in hysterics over the client, Mary Sutherland, who has lost her fiancé. Holmes rightly issues a rebuke, "This may be amusing to you, Watson, but it's something of a tragedy to that simple-minded girl!"; an authentic Watson would never have been so insensitive. The film requires a bogus character to fool those who know him well

Below, Eille Norwood's Sherlock Holmes breaks in on the forced wedding in *The Solitary Cyclist* (1921) and trains his gun on the villainous Woodley (Allan Jeayes) and his accomplices. The reluctant bride Violet (Violet Hewitt) comforts the young man, Bob Carruthers (R. D. Sylvester), who loves her.

Above, Sherlock Holmes (Eille Norwood) and Doctor Watson (Hubert Willis) have captured a youngish Colonel Sebastian Moran (Sidney Seaward) in the 1921 film, *The Empty House*.

under good lighting, and it is equally hard to believe the deception at the heart of *The Man with the Twisted Lip*, when the beggar suspected of murder can be so clearly seen. In *The Beryl Coronet*, Holmes no longer pays a fence to recover the missing gems, and he brings a curious morality to bear, insisting that the caddish Sir George Burnwell must marry the girl he has misled into stealing them as well as restoring the property. He is also given a new closing thought – "Their loves and hates are woven like the pattern of a Grieg sonata" – which Watson interprets as a cue to hand him the violin.

The feature-length *The Hound of the Baskervilles* is no better than the shorts. There is some unintentionally broad playing from Fred Raynham as Barrymore, a butler who seems to think he's in a comedy, and Lewis Gilbert as Stapleton, who behaves suspiciously on every appearance. The hound is suitably massive, but its fiery jowls appear to be the result of crude scratching on the negative. Holmes solves the case with far less difficulty than in the original story, spotting the portrait resemblance between Stapleton and the Baskerville line as soon as he walks into the house. Grimpen Mire, "a false step into which means certain death", crops up in the film only at the end when it is time for Stapleton to fall into it. Oddly, Holmes does not participate in rescuing Sir Henry from the hound's final attack but is instead attempting in vain to pull Stapleton out of the quagmire. The film reduces Beryl Stapleton's role in her husband's plot so that Sir Henry can still remain in love with her at the end. Holmes brings the story to a limp close by observing, "Love, my dear Watson, is perhaps a tonic to Sir Henry. Personally, I could do with a large whisky and soda."

Stoll's activity seems to have reawakened Conan Doyle's own interest in Sherlock Holmes, for he wrote a one-act play, *The Crown Diamond*, which was first performed in Bristol in May 1921 and staged elsewhere (including two separate one-week engagements at the London Coliseum) for over a year. In this play, Holmes (Dennis Neilson-Terry) receives a personal request from the Prime Minister and Home Secretary to recover the Crown Diamond. He first appears on stage disguised as an old woman and fools Watson (R. V. Taylour). Expecting to be shot at by Colonel Sebastian Moran, he arranges a life-size dummy of himself in the window (as in the story *The Empty House*). Colonel Moran calls on Holmes, who knows he has the diamond and offers to let him go free if it is safely returned. Moran discusses the proposal with a confederate after Holmes withdraws and is heard playing the violin – but in fact the sleuth has put on a record and substitutes himself for the dummy during a pre-arranged blackout to overhear Moran disclose the whereabouts of the diamond.

Sir Arthur put the story to further use by presenting it to *The Strand Magazine* as *The Adventure of the Mazarin Stone*. To differentiate it from *The Empty House*, he turned Moran into Count Negretto Sylvius. He also eliminated the blackout device, simply having Holmes slip into the room and exchange himself for the dummy, which is in plain view, making only the slightest of noises. It defies belief that Holmes could be sure Sylvius and his confederate would be looking the other way. Having recovered the missing gem, Holmes indulges his "impish habit of practical joking" by slipping it into the pocket of the pompous owner and threatening him with arrest for having received it – a feeble echo of his playful ways with clients in earlier stories. *The Adventure of the Mazarin Stone* is widely regarded as the worst of all the Holmes stories.

Holmes's creator was not opposed to providing the further occasional memoir, but he had difficulty in thinking up fresh ideas. He would sometimes purchase readers' suggestions or even fully-drafted stories if they had a good idea he might use in his own way later, and it was only thanks to the *Strand*'s editor, Greenhough Smith, who told him of a true case of a suicide disguised as murder, that Conan Doyle came up with *The Problem of Thor Bridge*, which was stretched over the February and March 1922 issues of the magazine. The author made excellent use of

Although one of the weakest stories, *The Adventure of the Mazarin Stone* was well illustrated by A. Gilbert in the *Strand* (October 1921). Here Sherlock Holmes interrupts Count Negretto Sylvius, who is about to strike the detective's life-size model.

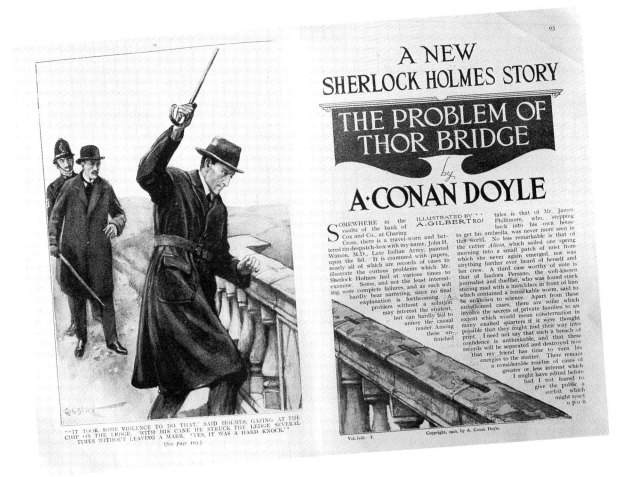

Readers opened the *Strand* for February 1922 to find at the beginning of *The Problem of Thor Bridge* this double-page spread with its interesting balance of text and picture. A. Gilbert's illustration shows Holmes striking the side of the bridge to test how much force was required to take a chip out of the stonework.

the idea in Watson's account of Holmes being engaged by an American millionaire to help a young governess accused of shooting his wife on a bridge in Hampshire.

Despite their faults, there had been a brisk demand for the films that Stoll had made, and another 15 shorts were screened for the trade in March 1922. George Ridgwell had succeeded Maurice Elvey as director while the adaptations were done by new writers, P. L. Mannock and Geoffrey H. Malins. This group was called *The Further Adventures of Sherlock Holmes*, and to judge by surviving examples they were a considerable improvement. The version of *The Musgrave Ritual*, for instance, is very faithful to the original story. Although it is inevitably condensed and Holmes solves the ritual too quickly, it is interesting that the entire catechism is carefully shown written out on the screen (the full version, too, including a couplet omitted from the *Strand* and many anthologies). The film might not impress a viewer unfamiliar with the story already, but it is an excellent digest and reminder, with much lengthier titles than in the first set of adaptations.

In contrast to Stoll's modest programme, a major new film version of the William Gillette stage play, *Sherlock Holmes*, was made by the Samuel Goldwyn company and received its American premiere on 1 May 1922. The screenwriters Marion Fairfax and Earle Browne added an ingenious opening section in which Holmes and Watson are shown as friends at Cambridge, and Holmes clears a fellow student, Prince Alexis, who has been accused of theft. The young Sherlock discovers that Professor Moriarty, already the Napoleon of crime, is behind it all and makes his acquaintance in a Limehouse den. The student sleuth also falls for beautiful Alice Faulkner at this time – she is the sister of Alexis's girlfriend, who commits suicide when the Prince discards her. All this provides a much stronger foundation from which to launch into the Gillette play.

With a lavish budget and the charismatic John Barrymore as Holmes, plus a powerful Moriarty in Gustav von Seyffertitz, this *Sherlock Holmes* could have been memorable; instead it is dully handled and plods along with far too many titles.

In another isolated addition to the stories, Conan Doyle wrote *The Adventure of the Creeping Man*. The solution to why an elderly, staid professor has twice been attacked by his devoted wolf-hound belongs more to the horror field, concerning as it does an elixir of youth with unfortunate side effects. The detection required of Holmes is very elementary indeed. With this story Howard Elcock became the *Strand*'s regular illustrator of Holmes, using a crayon style to create dark but incisive studies.

Stoll were now ready with *The Last Adventures of Sherlock Holmes*, another 15 shorts produced by George Ridgwell, plus a full-length *The Sign of Four*, directed by Maurice Elvey. Again the shorts are a painstaking and honest attempt to convey the outline of particular stories, but they rarely capture the full mood of a situation, and they are more interesting to Holmesians for their deviations and shortcuts. The coded messages in *The "Gloria Scott"* and *The Dancing Men* are faithfully reproduced, but Holmes is allowed to solve them unsatisfactorily, too quickly spotting the key to the first, and, of the latter's terpsichorean stick figures, airily declaring, "Having applied the rules which guide us in all forms of secret writings, the solution was fairly easy." In *The Missing Three-Quarter*, Dr Leslie Armstrong is nowhere near as menacing as he should be, provoking Holmes to describe him as "A most interesting personality, Watson!" instead of an incipient Moriarty, while the story's tragic outcome and Holmes's withdrawal are perfunctorily handled.

The ending of *The "Gloria Scott"* in which Holmes decides to burn the older Trevor's confession is perhaps sensible and in character, if not faithful to Conan Doyle, but *The Crooked Man* has an astonishing new happy ending in which Watson touches the crippled Henry Wood in a couple of places and immediately assures him, "Modern surgery will make you a new man", while Holmes informs the lady in the case that he will soon be ready for nursing after the operation.

Above, John Barrymore is Holmes, Gustav von Seyffertitz is a particularly horrific-looking Moriarty, and Jerry Devine is the pageboy Billy in the classic encounter as it appeared in the 1922 film, *Sherlock Holmes*. Left, Eille Norwood's Sherlock Holmes is helped by Hubert Willis's Dr Watson to raise the flagstone in *The Musgrave Ritual*, from the 1922 series *The Further Adventures of Sherlock Holmes*. Geoffrey Wilmer's Reginald Musgrave is on hand to see the mystery solved in the cellar beneath.

There are good impressions conveyed by Eille Norwood of Holmes working a week on the first ciphers of *The Dancing Men* or deliberating all night in *The Disappearance of Lady Frances Carfax*, but these films rush over important moments – a dully angled shot fails to convey the urgency with which Holmes awakens Watson after having rumbled the impending fate of Lady Frances, while in *His Last Bow* the concluding terrace scene has a severely abbreviated version of the "east wind" speech, delivered when Holmes pauses on some steps before hurrying on with Watson. *The Mystery of Thor Bridge* is unusual in the poetic licence taken by the title writer, describing Holmes as "the analyst of souls", referring to "the inexorable grindstone of fate" as the American millionaire is about to learn of his wife's death, and prefacing a shot of a prison entrance with the phrase "At the 'Gates of Despair'".

Budgetary restrictions have clipped the wings of some of the stories, although good Cambridge-seeming locations are evident in *The Missing Three-Quarter* and others have busy street scenes. However, *The Disappearance of Lady Frances Carfax* has a section relocated from the original's Hotel National at Lausanne to the Grand Hotel at Tungate Spa, England. And *The Final Problem* isn't quite the same when, instead of racing to Switzerland to elude Moriarty, Holmes tells Watson: "We will go to Cheddar for a few days." But *The Final Problem* is still a fairly commendable piece of work within the imposed limitations. There is an excellent Moriarty from Percy Standing, and the sharp verbal parries of the Baker Street encounter with Holmes are quite well conveyed by titles (Watson is, for once, a witness to the meeting and so knows for sure that Moriarty is all that Holmes has said), while Cheddar Gorge does prove a striking visual substitute for the Swiss Alps. Unfortunately the struggle between Holmes and Moriarty is filmed from such an angle that they seem to be rolling toward higher ground rather than a cliff edge. Watson's careless conversation has enabled Moriarty to track Holmes to Cheddar, and his anguish at the end, as he looks over the cliff edge after both men have fallen is, one hopes, tinged with a realization of his stupidity. (Oddly, the sequel *The*

As master spy Von Bork (Nelson Ramsay) picks up a book on bee culture instead of the British naval codes, Eille Norwood's Sherlock Holmes, disguised as an Irish-American in goatee beard, applies the chloroform in the 1923 film adaptation *His Last Bow* for the series *The Last Adventures of Sherlock Holmes*.

Moriarty (Percy Standing) again meets Holmes (Eille Norwood) at Baker Street in *The Final Problem* from the 1923 series *The Last Adventures of Sherlock Holmes*. Instead of the pageboy Billy, it is Watson (Hubert Willis, left) who is present at their tense discussion.

In Stoll's 1923 feature film *The Sign of Four*, with Eille Norwood as Holmes, Dr Watson (played by Arthur Cullin) has examined the body at Pondicherry Lodge and turns towards Mary Morstan (Isobel Elsom).

Empty House had been filmed in the first series.) For the feature *The Sign of Four*, Watson was played by the slightly younger Arthur Cullin, who had first played the Doctor in the recent film of *The Valley of Fear* and this permitted a more plausible romance with Isobel Elsom as Mary Morstan.

The Stoll company had filmed every short story up to and including *Thor Bridge* with the singular exception of *The Five Orange Pips*. The recent British films of *A Study in Scarlet* and *The Valley of Fear* prevented Stoll from re-making those novels but the remaining two, *The Hound of the Baskervilles* and *The Sign of Four*, had been undertaken. Eille Norwood was reluctant to give up Holmes and played him on the stage, producing as well as starring in *The Return of Sherlock Holmes*, written by his nephew J. E. Harold-Terry with Arthur Rose and approved by Conan Doyle. The production was based on a number of the short stories, especially *The Disappearance of Lady Frances Carfax*, but it also drew on the Gillette play for the action highlight of Holmes's escape from a criminal den. It had a successful London run from October 1923, and Eille Norwood toured with the play in the provinces the following year.

The next few years were devoid of new Sherlock Holmes films. There were occasional new stories appearing in the *Strand* but they were far inferior to Conan Doyle's earlier work. They maintained interest in Holmes but did nothing to enhance his reputation.

The Adventure of the Sussex Vampire (1924) exemplifies the somewhat fantastical titles with which, as Holmes once noted, Watson was fond of embellishing his accounts. Although it seems at first that the story falls into the horror genre, Holmes is contemptuous of the vampire legend from the start: "Rubbish, Watson, rubbish! What have we to do with walking corpses who can only be held in their grave by

A series of 25 cigarette cards featuring Conan Doyle's characters was issued in 1923 with packets of Turf cigarettes by Alexander Bogulavsky. All but six of the cards showed figures from the Sherlock Holmes stories. Here is Holmes himself and the other characters chosen from various of the stories.

stakes driven through their hearts? It's pure lunacy." So why was Robert Ferguson's wife found apparently biting the neck of her infant boy? Holmes quickly and masterfully solves the problem, exposing in the crippled son disturbed by his father's re-marriage one of the most repulsive characters in the entire *œuvre*. The mistreatment of a dog provides a clue in the manner that lame sheep did in *Silver Blaze*.

In the same year *The Book of the Queen's Dolls' House Library* was published. This contained a number of famous authors' hand-written contributions in miniature blank books for the dolls' house of Queen Mary. Sir Arthur provided a very short parody, *How Watson Learned the Trick*, in which the doctor tries to read Sherlock Holmes's mind at the breakfast table – and is hopelessly wrong.

More weighty was the book *Memories and Adventures*, which collected together various reminiscences that Conan Doyle had written of his life for *The Strand Magazine* between 1897 and 1923, together with some new linking material. It included his own account of how he created Holmes.

Two more Holmes stories were first published in 1924. If *The Adventure of the Three Garridebs* rather obviously repeats the plot mechanism of *The Red-Headed League*, the result is once again diverting. Here the apparent key to good fortune is being named Garrideb rather than possessing red hair. Holmes makes his first recorded use of the telephone in this investigation. The American villain Killer Evans proves to be more dangerous than Holmes anticipates, firing his gun and wounding Watson. The doctor records Holmes's concern:

"You're not hurt, Watson? For God's sake, say that you are not hurt!"

It was worth a wound – it was worth many wounds – to know the depth of loyalty and love which lay behind that cold mask. The clear, hard eyes were dimmed for a moment, and the firm lips were shaking. For the one and only time I caught a glimpse of a great heart as well as of a great brain. All my years of humble but single-minded service culminated in that moment of revelation.

Fortunately, Watson's wound is superficial but Holmes sounds convincing when he tells Evans: "If you had killed Watson, you would not have got out of this room alive." Holmes's error was surely in not having police support after setting the trap for Evans.

In *The Adventure of the Illustrious Client*, it is Holmes's turn to be injured – by minions of the heinous wife murderer Baron Adelbert Gruner who reduce the detective to his worst physical state in any of the recorded adventures. Watson wants to thrash the hide off Gruner, prompting Holmes to say "Good old Watson!", a rare use of what became a catchphrase in later movies. Holmes, preferring a more subtle method of dealing with the Baron, has Watson masquerade as an expert on Chinese pottery (typically without explaining the reason). Gruner is another of the canon's learned villains: Moriarty was an author and mathematician of note, and Gruner is a writer and authority on Chinese pottery. While Watson engages Gruner's attention, Holmes breaks in to steal a diary from the next room, a further example of his practical, if unlawful, methods. Conan Doyle regarded this story highly, and in 1926 he declared that it was among the six best.

But his major literary effort at this period was *The Land of Mist*, serialized in *The Strand Magazine* and published in book form in March 1926. It was a psychic novel, based on Conan Doyle's own experiences, in which he depicted the slow conversion of Professor Challenger, the leading figure in *The Lost World*, from a sceptic to a believer in spiritualism. It is interesting that Conan Doyle did not convert Sherlock Holmes to the cause. Was it because he felt that Holmes could never have convinced readers, or was it an expression of a greater fondness for Challenger that he had the glory of becoming a spiritualist. The last six Holmes stories that were delivered to *Liberty* and *The Strand Magazine* suggest that he had really lost interest in his

The climax of *The Adventure of the Three Garridebs*, as illustrated by Howard K. Elcock in the January 1925 issue of *The Strand Magazine*. Killer Evans emerges from the trap door to be confronted by Watson and Holmes. After Evans has whisked out a gun and wounded Watson, Holmes brings his pistol down on the man's head instead of firing back.

Sherlock Holmes is rarely mentioned using the telephone, but he is seen here with the instrument in Howard K. Elcock's illustration from *The Adventure of the Three Garridebs* (*Strand*, January 1925).

Most vintage copies of *The Strand Magazine* seem to survive in bound volumes without the covers. Here, as it would have been first seen by readers, is a rare glimpse of the November 1926 issue with its promise of a brand-new Sherlock Holmes adventure.

creation. They can be placed among the bottom ten of the canon without much fear of provoking argument.

Among them, *The Adventure of the Three Gables* is a positive embarrassment, as Holmes directs crude racist gibes at a black boxer turned thug (in contrast to his compassion towards a black child in *The Yellow Face*). The poor dialogue and feeble plot make the story most unrewarding.

Conan Doyle tried having Holmes relate two stories himself. After criticizing Watson so often for emphasizing lurid details rather than demonstrating the logic and science of his methods, Holmes proceeds to write in a style and approach indistinguishable from that of his biographer instead of providing sample chapters of the volume that (in *The Abbey Grange*) he promised to write on the art of detection. Neither case is a brilliant example of his powers.

In *The Adventure of the Blanched Soldier*, Holmes has little difficulty gaining access to the elusive Godfrey Emsworth, but he withholds from us the magic word that he writes on a slip of paper so as to prolong interest in the story instead of sharing his deduction. The conclusion is unexpectedly happy, although something of an anti-climax.

As much of a let-down is the solution to *The Adventure of the Lion's Mane*. When a man and later his dog are killed on a beach, seemingly flogged to death, the case looks mystifyingly complex, but the solution is based on Holmes's omniverous reading and retentive memory rather than his deductive skills (although again he keeps us in the dark, as if we were Watson). The story is of some interest in being placed during Holmes's retirement to bee-keeping on the South Downs (hence no Watson to record the case). The ageing Holmes was poorly depicted in the *Strand* by Howard Elcock. Hereafter the excellent Frank Wiles returned as illustrator.

Watson is amply present during *The Adventure of the Retired Colourman*, being dispatched by Holmes to investigate the disappearance of Josiah Amberley's young

wife and her doctor friend at Lewisham. Watson's account records even worse treatment from Holmes than normal: he has "missed everything of importance" as usual and Holmes tries to soothe him by saying "Don't be hurt, my dear fellow. You know that I am quite impersonal. No one else would have done better. Some possibly not so well." Does Holmes *have* to be "impersonal" with such an old friend, and be quite so rude as to suggest that hardly anyone could have done worse? Poor old Watson! And then he is made by Holmes to share an overnight trip with the tedious, miserly Amberley without being taken into Holmes's confidence (as usual). Watson returns in a foul temper to learn that Holmes has apparently acquired a new assistant called Barker (confusingly, Holmes says that Barker is working on the case independently and also that he "has done nothing save what I told him"). It will hardly spoil such a limp tale to note that it is the only instance in which the villain brings Holmes into the case, a course recommended by Scotland Yard and failure to do so might have aroused suspicion.

This was the second shortest of all the 60 stories, another sign of the creator's flagging interest, and the next was the shortest of all. *The Adventure of the Veiled Lodger* requires no deduction by Holmes; he simply listens to the confession of Angela Ronder, whose face was torn apart by a lion. His only active role is to dissuade her from suicide. It would have been much more interesting to read "the whole story concerning the politician, the lighthouse, and the trained cormorant", to which Watson alludes in his opening remarks!

Conan Doyle delayed the appearance of the very last story that he would ever write about the greatest of all detectives by setting "A Sherlock Holmes Competition" for readers of the *Strand*. From the 44 stories so far published in book form, he selected his choice of the best 12 and challenged readers to match his list. After they had had time to submit their guesses, Sir Arthur revealed his dozen together with his reasons.

The Adventure of the Illustrious Client was first published in America in *Collier's* issue dated 8 November 1924 and this large illustration drawn by John Richard Flanagan appeared at the head of the story. It shows the wounded Holmes providing Watson with a valuable Ming dynasty saucer to help the doctor masquerade as a collector and gain access to the villain's inner sanctum. Holmes looks like a square-jawed Hollywood leading man in the Richard Dix tradition.

Frederic Dorr Steele provided this eloquent study of the ageing detective deep in thought on the shore for *Liberty Magazine*'s publication of *The Adventure of the Lion's Mane* in its issue of 27 November 1926.

The ageing detective of *Lion's Mane* is seen here in one of seven murals created by Robin Jaques for display at Baker Street Underground Station in London. This is the retired Holmes, watched by a neighbour called Harold Stackhurst, contemplating the body of a man who has just died mysteriously. The murals are to be found on the Jubilee Line platforms 7 (southbound) and 10 (northbound).

This attractive study by Frank Wiles shows
Sherlock Holmes listening to Watson's account
of his investigation into the disappearance of
Josiah Amberley's wife in *The Adventure of the
Retired Colourman*. Holmes tells Watson to cut
out the poetry and stick to the facts. From the
Strand, January 1927.

There is the grim snake story, *The Speckled Band*. That I am sure will be on
every list. Next to that in popular favour and in my own esteem I would place
The Red-Headed League and *The Dancing Men*, on account in each case of the
originality of the plot. Then we could hardly leave out the story which deals
with the only foe who ever really extended Holmes, and which deceived the
public (and Watson) into the erroneous inference of his death. Also, I think the
first story of all should go in, as it opened the path for the others, and as it has
more female interest than is usual. Finally, I think the story which essays the
difficult task of explaining away the alleged death of Holmes, and which also
introduces such a villain as Colonel Sebastian Moran, should have a place. This
puts *The Final Problem*, *A Scandal in Bohemia* and *The Empty House* upon our
list, and we have got our first half-dozen.

But now comes the crux. There are a number of stories which really are a
little hard to separate. On the whole I think I should find a place for *The Five
Orange Pips*. So now only five places are left. There are two stories which deal
with high diplomacy and intrigue. They are both among the very best of the
series. The one is *The Naval Treaty* and the other *The Second Stain*. There is no
room for both of them in the team, and on the whole I regard the latter as the
better story. Therefore we will put it down for the eighth place.

And now which? *The Devil's Foot* has points. It is grim and new. We will
give it the ninth place. I think also that *The Priory School* is worth a place if only
for the dramatic moment when Holmes points his finger at the Duke. I have
only two places left. I hesitate between *Silver Blaze*, *The Bruce-Partington
Plans*, *The Crooked Man*, *The Man With The Twisted Lip*, *The "Gloria Scott"*,
The Greek Interpreter, *The Reigate Squires*, *The Musgrave Ritual*, and *The
Resident Patient*. On what principle am I to choose two out of these? The racing
detail in *Silver Blaze* is very faulty, so we must disqualify him. There is little to
choose between the others. A small thing would turn the scale. *The Musgrave
Ritual* has a historical touch which gives it a little added distinction. It is also a
memory from Holmes's early life. So now we come to the very last. I might as
well draw the name out of a bag, for I see no reason to put one before the other.

The departing Sherlock Holmes turns back to advise against suicide in *The Adventure of the Veiled Lodger* after hearing Angela Ronder's tragic story. A Frank Wiles illustration from the *Strand*, February 1927.

This 1926 *Punch* cartoon by Bernard Partridge sums up Sir Arthur's feelings of being taken over by his creation.

Whatever their merit – and I make no claim for that – they are all as good as I could make them. On the whole Holmes himself shows perhaps most ingenuity in *The Reigate Squires* and therefore this shall be twelfth man in my team.

He added that, had his latest stories been included, he would have chosen *The Lion's Mane* and *The Illustrious Client*. These and *The Five Orange Pips* are not highly regarded by Holmesians today.*

The sixtieth and final problem was *The Adventure of Shoscombe Old Place*. Holmes

* A good indication of how the stories settled down in esteem is provided by the *Baker Street Journal's* well-supported poll of readers in 1959, when the top 10 short stories were *The Speckled Band* (278 votes), *The Red-Headed League* (234), *The Blue Carbuncle* and *Silver Blaze* (both 199), *A Scandal in Bohemia* (172), *The Musgrave Ritual* (149), *The Bruce-Partington Plans* (114), *The Six Napoleons* (101), *The Dancing Men* (88) and *The Empty House* (79). The least favourite 10 were (in order of disdain) *The Mazarin Stone* (208 votes), *The Veiled Lodger* (201), *The Yellow Face* (193), *The Blanched Soldier* (168), *The Three Gables* (139), *The Creeping Man* (107), *The Retired Colourman* (101), *The Lion's Mane* (82), *The Sussex Vampire* (73) and *The Missing Three-Quarter* (69). Regrettably, the *Baker Street Journal* has not polled readers in recent years. (This American quarterly of Sherlockian debate and speculation is currently published by Fordham University Press, University Box L, Bronx, NY 100458, USA.)

Dressed as usual in his deerstalker for country work, Sherlock Holmes asks Sir Robert Norberton to explain the body he has found in the crypt. Frank Wiles contributed this vivid illustration to the *Strand*'s April 1927 issue when the last of Conan Doyle's stories, *The Adventure of Shoscombe Old Place*, appeared.

again has little to do. His night-time visit to the crypt of Shoscombe Old Place, seeking to unravel the strange conduct of Sir Robert Norberton, is interrupted by the peppery knight's arrival to provide his own explanation.

The last 12 stories were published collectively as *The Case Book of Sherlock Holmes*, somewhat re-arranged from their order of first appearance. The introduction showed that Conan Doyle's resentment of his creation had waned:

> Had Holmes never existed I could not have done more, though he may perhaps have stood a little in the way of the recognition of my more serious literary work. And so, reader, farewell to Sherlock Holmes! I thank you for your past constancy and can but hope that some return has been made in the shape of that distraction from the worries of life and stimulating change of thought which can only be found in the fairy kingdom of romance.

By now new detectives were on the literary scene with modern styles and modern methods. Agatha Christie's Hercule Poirot, Dorothy L. Sayers' Lord Peter Wimsey, S.S. Van Dine's Philo Vance, Earl Derr Biggers' Charlie Chan and others had started their careers.

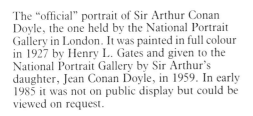

Sir Arthur's grave at Minstead in the New Forest of Hampshire. The Minstead area featured prominently in his novel *The White Company*, which is set in medieval times.

The "official" portrait of Sir Arthur Conan Doyle, the one held by the National Portrait Gallery in London. It was painted in full colour in 1927 by Henry L. Gates and given to the National Portrait Gallery by Sir Arthur's daughter, Jean Conan Doyle, in 1959. In early 1985 it was not on public display but could be viewed on request.

Conan Doyle mostly lived in seclusion in the New Forest near Minstead, where he was viewed with suspicion because of his spiritualist beliefs. But he emerged for speaking engagements as well as to further the cause of the long-imprisoned Oscar Slater, providing the introduction to a new book that revived public interest and secured his release. In late 1928 and early 1929, Conan Doyle made a long tour of Africa with his wife and sons Denis and Adrian (then called Malcolm). In autumn 1929 he went to Scandinavia to lecture on spiritualism, but his health was now poor and on 7 July 1930 he died at his main home at Crowborough. He was buried in the grounds. When the property was sold, his earthly remains (with those of his wife Jean, who died on 27 June 1940) were moved to Minstead Church near the other house he had bought at Bignell Wood. On the southern edge of the churchyard will be found his tombstone with its inscription:

STEEL TRUE

BLADE STRAIGHT

ARTHUR CONAN DOYLE

KNIGHT

PATRIOT, PHYSICIAN AND MAN OF LETTERS

Besides his wife and sons, he was survived by his creation, Sherlock Holmes. The man he had once wished to see dead would ensure that his own name remained alive for generations to come.

Brother Mycroft, followed by Inspector Lestrade, arrives at Baker Street to involve Sherlock Holmes in *The Adventure of the Bruce-Partington Plans* (*Strand*, December 1908). Arthur Twidle provides an alternative depiction of Mycroft and Lestrade to those by Paget reproduced on pages 30 and 46.

8 SHERLOCK HOLMES IN THE THIRTIES

Before his death, Sir Arthur had both witnessed and participated in the arrival of talking motion pictures. He gave a newsreel interview, and the soft voice emanating from his huge, but now frail, form still carried the accent of Edinburgh as he talked about Sherlock Holmes and spiritualism, and he had also been filmed making a speech about his belief in life after death, leaving a record of what a fluent and skilful orator he was.

There was a last silent film – another German version of *The Hound of the Baskervilles* with an international cast (the American actor Carlyle Blackwell played Holmes) – before a spate of sound pictures began, although Paramount bridged the gap with *The Return of Sherlock Holmes*, which was made at the company's New York studios and shot in both silent and talking versions. The studio purchased the right to use Conan Doyle's characters and devised an original plot (the work of American writer Garrett Fort and Basil Dean, a Briton who also directed). Clive Brook portrayed Holmes; H. Reeves Smith was Watson; Donald Crisp was Colonel Moran; and Harry T. Morey was Moriarty.

The bulk of the story was set on an ocean liner. Moriarty has kidnapped the boyfriend of Watson's daughter on the eve of their marriage and put him in a cabin on the ship; Holmes and Watson come on board, hot on the trail, and Holmes

In *The Return of Sherlock Holmes* (1929), Sherlock Holmes (Clive Brook) pretends to have succumbed to poison and fools Moriarty (Harry T. Morey).

disguises himself as a violinist (what else?) in the ship's orchestra and as a cabin steward to help locate the missing man; at the climax, Moriarty and Holmes dine together and Moriarty attempts to kill the detective with a poisoned thorn in a cigarette case. The film was made in the early days of sound when directors with theatrical experience were favoured to help actors manage dialogue. Unfortunately they too often knew little about cinema techniques, and camera mobility was very restricted, the equipment being placed in a glass-fronted, soundproof booth while speech was recorded. Contemporary reviews indicate that the film was not well received by critics, and it has not yet been revived for television, although it survives.

Clive Brook played Holmes again for a short burlesque sequence in *Paramount on Parade*; he appeared with William Powell, playing another popular detective, Philo Vance, and with Warner Oland, playing the evil Fu Manchu. The sketch concludes with Holmes's death. Paramount had no plans to resurrect Holmes for further films.

In 1930 American radio began a series of 35 weekly broadcasts of adaptations by Edith Meiser of the original short stories. William Gillette (then in the midst of a lengthy farewell tour in his celebrated play) performed in the first, *The Speckled Band*, but Richard Gordon took over for the rest of the series. Leigh Lovell was the voice of Dr Watson. A second series of broadcasts followed in 1931–2 with Gordon and Lovell, but writer Edith Meiser was forced to concoct some original stories, such as *The Missing Leonardo da Vinci*, and to detail cases that Dr Watson had mentioned only in passing, such as *The Giant Rat of Sumatra*, an affair for which the world was not yet prepared when it was alluded to in *The Sussex Vampire*.

A third series, broadcast in 1932–3, was even more dependent on new material, and Edith Meiser concocted solutions to more tantalisingly unchronicled cases like *The Singular Affair of the Aluminium Crutch*. (Gordon and Lovell were seen as actors playing Holmes and Watson in a Universal two-reeler of 1933, *The Radio Murder Mystery*.) For the 1934–5 season, Louis Hector replaced Gordon, although Leigh Lovell continued as Watson, and entirely original material by Edith Meiser seems to have been used. (Hector became the first actor to play Holmes on television in a live transmission from New York of *The Three Garridebs* in 1937.)

Back in the cinema, three different actors essayed Holmes in British productions of the early 1930s. The Canadian-born Raymond Massey made his screen debut playing the sleuth, with Athole Stewart as Watson, in *The Speckled Band*, based on Conan Doyle's story and theatre adaptation (Lyn Harding repeated his stage work as the film's Dr Grimesby Rylott). Robert Rendel was Holmes in a Gainsborough version of *The Hound of the Baskervilles*, for which Edgar Wallace wrote the dialogue. Unfortunately, the soundtrack is reported lost and only the visuals of this film are definitely known to survive, but Rendel certainly looks physically miscast for the part. And then there was Arthur Wontner whose characterization of Holmes was simply masterly.

Wontner was in his mid-fifties when he first played Holmes in the 1931 release, *The Sleeping Cardinal*. He had the voice, looks and presence to be totally convincing as Holmes, although it was necessarily an ageing Holmes, one more sedate and less physically active but with exactly the right pensive manner. The tall, thin Wontner is closer to the illustrations of Holmes in *The Strand Magazine* than any other actor has been. Like Eille Norwood, he was really too old to play the practising detective of the stories because Conan Doyle had retired Holmes around the age of fifty but, if Holmes had continued in practice, this is how one imagines he would have looked. His age has made him more indulgent towards the lesser minds of Watson and Lestrade, and there is more of a feeling of respect for Watson (played efficiently and unflamboyantly by Ian Fleming) than in many later screen depictions of the pair. In *The Sleeping Cardinal*, Mrs Hudson (stoutly portrayed by Minnie Rayner) figures larger than usual in life at 221B Baker Street, and she enjoys a rather more friendly, informal relationship with Holmes, again as though the old reserve has melted over the years.

Robert Rendel (left) as Holmes, Frederick Lloyd (centre) as Watson and Wilfred Shine as Dr Mortimer in the 1932 production of *The Hound of the Baskervilles*.

Dr Grimesby Rylott (Lyn Harding) threatens Raymond Massey's Sherlock Holmes in the 1931 screen version of *The Speckled Band*. Another bald Watson, played by Athole Stewart, observes.

The plot of *The Sleeping Cardinal* twists the story of *The Empty House* to make the card-playing Ronald Adair a cheat. He is blackmailed by a hidden Moriarty, who talks to him from behind a wall on which there is a picture of a sleeping cardinal (hence the film's British title; it was renamed *Sherlock Holmes' Fatal Hour* for American release). Moriarty conceals his face when he visits Holmes at Baker Street (a scene based on the meeting in *The Final Problem*), and his subterfuge is necessary because he is masquerading as one of the other characters in the film. Also taken from *The Empty House* is the sequence of a shot being fired at Sherlock Holmes's silhouette in the window of Baker Street, but here the would-be assassin is Moriarty, not Colonel Moran (who features in the film as a henchman).

There are touches also from the Gillette play. "Elementary, my dear Watson!" is frequently heard, after the good doctor compliments Holmes on his deductive powers, and Moriarty is given the first name Robert (as in the original play) rather than James (as in Conan Doyle.) (The current acting edition of the play has been changed to follow Conan Doyle.)

The Sleeping Cardinal was well received, and Arthur Wontner's performance gained the accolades it deserved. The film was made by independent producer

Julius Hagen at the small Twickenham Studios, and he soon had a second Holmes feature, *The Missing Rembrandt*, in production with Wontner and the same director, Leslie S. Hiscott, and screenwriters, Cyril Twyford and H. Fowler Mear, as the first. Loosely based on *Charles Augustus Milverton*, the film turned the society blackmailer into a wealthy art dealer, Baron von Guntermann, played by Francis L. Sullivan, whose activities include stealing a Rembrandt from the Louvre and gathering compromising letters from a society lady. *The Missing Rembrandt* is also a missing film (British television would like to show it), but it was praised in contemporary reviews.

Wontner was recruited to play Holmes again by the larger Associated Radio Pictures. *The Sign of Four* was made with Graham Cutts directing and Hollywood's Rowland V. Lee as production supervisor. The American influence was strong, with a Hollywood cinematographer and editor, and the film tried to reach a wider audience than the two Julius Hagen productions. Wontner was given a toupee to

A first-class Holmes: Arthur Wontner (1875–1960). This portrait, taken for *The Sign of Four* (1932), shows him with a toupee.

cover his balding head, although he still had a strongly receding hairline as in the *Strand* illustrations. As in the 1923 version, Watson was played by a much younger actor, Ian Hunter, to make the wooing of Mary Morstan more appealing (he pesters her at every opportunity as an older Watson could never have done). Screenwriter W.P. Lipscomb moved the long flashback to the front of the film, delaying Holmes's first appearance. Although this device avoids interrupting the case later on, it explains too soon what is going on. Lipscomb also had the detective make some completely absurd deductions, such as declaring from the handwriting on a letter that its author has only one leg. (This Holmes has written a treatise on the physical and mental reactions of the disabled, and he tells us that an amputated leg leads to an increase in the pressure on the downstroke of a pen.) Holmes also deduces from the unusual scoring of Mary Morstan's fingers that she works in a flowershop and divines from a piece of rope that it is from a speedboat at a malt-unloading wharf, where there is a fighting climax with Holmes entering the fray. Wontner dons two disguises and twice utters the by now obligatory "Elementary my dear Watson, elementary". It is all too calculated to please, too glossy and slick, and it is hard to forgive the pointless change of address to 222A Baker Street.

Disguised as a sea salt, Sherlock Holmes (Arthur Wontner) teases information from a likely source in the 1932 film, *The Sign of Four*.

Fox's Hollywood production, *Sherlock Holmes* (1932), suffered from a similar attempt to widen its appeal. The company borrowed Clive Brook from Paramount to play Holmes again. Bertram Millhauser's script took over where Gillette's play left off. Moriarty has been sentenced to hang; Sherlock Holmes wants to marry Alice Faulkner, just as soon as a special licence can be obtained, and give up detective work. Fortunately, Moriarty escapes and sets about framing Holmes for the murder of a Scotland Yard rival, Gore-King, a scheme that assumes Holmes would shoot an intruder first and ask questions afterwards. Thinking Holmes out of the way, Moriarty kidnaps Alice and attempts to rob her father's bank in a manner suggested by *The Red-Headed League*.

There is none of the traditional Baker Street atmosphere. Holmes's quarters are dominated by a huge chemical laboratory. He has been updated from a consulting detective to a "scientific criminologist" who invents a device for disabling a fleeing car. Reginald Owen's Watson is reduced to a couple of appearances, and his place is taken elsewhere by the obnoxiously loud page-boy Billy who is being trained by Holmes in detective work.

And Clive Brook was quite wrong for the role of Sherlock Holmes The part can be played only by a character actor of no fixed identity who can shape himself to the role as Arthur Wontner did. Clive Brook was a star with a set image – and an unusually narrow range to boot. With his clipped, mannered accent, he was the epitome of the laid-back, stiff-upper-lip aristocratic Englishman, and he played Holmes as such. It is difficult to imagine this Holmes lying flat on the ground studying footprints. He moves in society circles – this Alice seems to have little other than breeding to recommend her – and his married life will include riding to hounds.

Brook introduced as much droll humour to the part as possible. He even sends up the line "Elementary, my dear Watson, elementary", speaking it in a gently mocking tone. He never wears the deerstalker and cape, and it is as though the traditional image of Holmes is one that embarrasses him. At the end of the film, Watson is inexcusably absent, and Holmes has to revise his catchphrase to "Elementary, my dear Billy, elementary", before kissing Alice to close the picture. This is a supercilious, dilettantish figure who is never a real Sherlock Holmes.

Yet, as a film, this *Sherlock Holmes* is of considerable interest. Ernest Torrence makes a splendidly commanding Moriarty whose threats, uttered with mock humility, demand to be taken seriously. He deserves the respect that Holmes shows for him, describing him as "a marvellous man" and underrating him in the comment that "While not a genius, he had the ability to stimulate genius in others", an adaptation of the remark once made by Holmes regarding Watson's luminosity. The production is strikingly shot, with some memorable wordless scenes built around Moriarty and based on silhouettes and shadows. This is a brisk and entertaining success on any basis of judgement other than as a Sherlock Holmes movie.

The film's vestigial Watson, Reginald Owen, was a Holmesian addict of long standing: as a child, he had lined up, his shilling in his hand, to obtain the latest instalment of *The Hound of the Baskervilles* from the *Strand* office on the day of publication. He managed to persuade a minor Hollywood studio, with the major-sounding name of World Wide, to make a Sherlock Holmes film for which, with Robert Florey, he devised the script and played the great detective himself, thus becoming the first actor to portray both Watson and Holmes.

Called *A Study in Scarlet*, the 1933 release had nothing to do with that story. Owen reportedly has some success in overcoming his unsuitably stocky appearance, thanks to his own well-written dialogue. In this film, too, Watson (played by Warburton Gamble) had little to do. Alan Mowbray, who played Scotland Yard's Gore-King in the last picture, here took on the traditional role of Inspector Lestrade, portraying him in tetchy humour. The principal villain, a jewel thief

A spot of tea in the laboratory. Reginald Owen's Dr Watson swaps pleasantries with Miriam Jordan's Alice Faulkner while Clive Brook's Sherlock Holmes stands aloof. A scene from the film *Sherlock Holmes* (1932).

Reginald Owen graduated from playing
Watson to become Holmes in *A Study in Scarlet*
(1933). Later actors who have played both roles
are Carleton Hobbs (British radio), Howard
Marion Crawford (British radio, American TV
series) and Jeremy Brett (American stage,
British television).

called Merrydew, could be the "Merridew of abominable memory" recorded in Holmes's commonplace book (and mentioned in *The Empty House*); and one of the gang is Jabez Wilson, the name given to the pawnbroker of *The Red-Headed League*, an unlikely convert to crime.

A new play of 1933 was Basil Mitchell's *The Holmeses of Baker Street*, whose awkward title imitated the hugely popular *The Barretts of Wimpole Street*. Mitchell had the extravagant idea of giving Sherlock Holmes a daughter, Shirley, who has inherited powers of deduction and wants to become the first woman detective at Scotland Yard!* When the play was first tried out at Edinburgh, there was even a prologue in which the happily-married Shirley nurses Sherlock Holmes's grandson. Felix Aylmer was rather dry casting for the super-sleuth 25 years into his retirement to keep bees in Sussex. His marriage, it seems, was ruined by his deductive bent and he wants his daughter to marry quickly and settle down to being a good wife.

The play brings him to London and a reunion with the John H. Watsons. Shirley and Mrs Watson connive to keep Holmes in London by faking the theft of a queen bee. Jewel thieves are brought into the plot and the setting reverts to Holmes's residence on the South Downs. The play was too far removed from audiences's expectations of a Sherlock Holmes adventure to be successful, although it toured for several months after a short West End run. It was also adapted for Broadway, where the perky screen actress Helen Chandler played Shirley to Cyril Scott's Sherlock. In this version, Shirley succeeded in becoming a detective at the Yard. The approach seems to have been more comically inclined but the play was short-lived.

With the realization that Conan Doyle's death completed the canon, there were the beginnings of scholarly activity to dissect and celebrate the achievement that was Sherlock Holmes. Books began appearing, like H.W. Bell's *Sherlock Holmes and Doctor Watson: The Chronology of their Adventures* (1932), which tackled the problem of arranging the adventures (chronicled and unchronicled) in the order they happened rather than their order of publication. In 1934, Sherlock Holmes societies were started in London and New York. The London society was really a dining club which intended to meet annually for dinner on Derby night, but after a couple of years members were advised in a typewritten communication that "The Sherlock Holmes Society, like the Red-Headed League, is dissolved." And it was not until 1951 that a new Sherlock Holmes Society of London was formed. The Baker Street Irregulars of New York, on the other hand, have continued uninterrupted to the present: membership is by invitation. Various scion societies have also become established in the United States, such as the Six Napoleons of Baltimore and the Red Circle of Washington D.C.

Arthur Wontner made his fourth appearance at Baker Street in the 1935 release, *The Triumph of Sherlock Holmes*, which reunited him with the team behind his first two films. Instead of a toupee, the writers accepted Wontner's ageing looks and had Holmes about to retire to the South Downs. Before he can leave Baker Street, however, he is visited by Professor Moriarty for yet another reprise of that encounter in *The Final Problem*, but it is as enjoyable as ever to hear the sharp dialogue exchanges, especially when players as effective as Wontner and, as Moriarty, Lyn Harding (who had earlier played Grimesby Rylott), are speaking the lines.

The film is really a very accurate and often satisfying version of *The Valley of Fear*, with Holmes lured from his retirement to look into the tragedy at Birlstone Manor. The long flashback to events in the American mining valley is awkwardly staged,

---

* Although Holmes said in *The Sign of Four* that he would never marry, he did not entirely rule out marriage and children. In the context of a wife's behaviour in *The Valley of Fear*, he declared: "Should I ever marry, Watson, I should hope to inspire my wife with some feeling that would prevent her from being walked off by a housekeeper when my corpse was lying within a few yards of her." And a client's son in *The Adventure of the Beryl Coronet*, Holmes remarked, "has carried himself in this matter as I should be proud to see my own son do, should I ever chance to have one".

Three scenes from the excellent 1935 film *The Triumph of Sherlock Holmes* with Arthur Wontner as Sherlock Holmes. Left, the meeting with Professor Moriarty (Lyn Harding). Centre, Watson (Ian Fleming) examines the corpse with the tattooed wrist at Birlstone Manor, watched by Holmes. Below, the capture of Moriarty at the Manor. The sceptical, bowler-hatted Inspector Lestrade (Charles Mortimer) is forced to admit that Moriarty really is the villainous mastermind claimed by Holmes. A moment later, the Professor breaks free and dashes away up the stairs, just visible in the right foreground – hardly the most intelligent direction of escape!

and the film offers a more dramatic climax by having Moriarty arrive, intending to pick up his assassin from a hiding place in the Manor house. It is not clear why Moriarty should personally bother with such a routine task or how Holmes knows he is due, but it makes for a pictorially splendid climax with a fierce struggle between Holmes and Moriarty, the latter losing another of his nine or more lives as he plunges from the customary great height. However, the scenes of Holmes's calm investigation are the most accomplished of the film, capturing the spirit and essence of the original story.

In America, at the age of 82, William Gillette starred in the Lux Radio Theatre's broadcast on 18 November 1935 of an adaptation of his play, *Sherlock Holmes*. Richard Gordon was again the Holmes of the weekly radio adaptations, but Harry West was a new Dr Watson.

Arthur Wontner made his final screen appearance as the great detective in *Silver Blaze*, another excellent Julius Hagen production, which was released in 1937. Lyn Harding re-appeared as Moriarty, having become the brains behind the abduction of the champion racehorse Silver Blaze. Colonel Sebastian Moran was also on hand, attempting to shoot the animal during the climactic race to add a new dramatic twist. To further expand the story into a feature-length film, Sir Henry Baskerville was introduced, inviting Holmes and Watson (Ian Fleming) to visit him in Devon and thereby bringing them into the vicinity of the case.

Like Gillette, Wontner's last performance as Holmes was on the radio: he starred in a 1943 BBC adaptation of *The Boscombe Valley Mystery* with, as his Watson, Carleton Hobbs, who would soon become *the* Sherlock Holmes of British broadcasting. It is gratifying to note that Wontner's fine interpretation was recognized by the new Sherlock Holmes Society of London, when he was the guest of honour at the annual dinner in 1955. (Carleton Hobbs is the only other actor to have been similarly invited.)

German enthusiasm for Holmes resurfaced spectacularly in 1937 when three films were made as part of a general liking for British crime subjects, with other subjects like Edgar Wallace's *The Ringer* being filmed in Germany. A third German version of *The Hound of the Baskervilles*, which starred Bruno Güttner as Holmes and Fritz Odemar as Watson, had as one of its keenest admirers Adolf Hitler, who acquired a print for his private collection. A film called *Die Graue Dame* (*The Green Lady*) pepped up the play on which it was based by adding Sherlock Holmes. And there was the ingenious and charming *Der Mann, Der Sherlock Holmes War* (*The Man Who Was Sherlock Holmes*), in which two seedy private detectives masquerade as Holmes and Watson, much to the hearty amusement of a burly Britisher who turns out to be none other than Sir Arthur Conan Doyle. It has become one of the classics of German film comedy.

In 1938, the young theatrical genius Orson Welles adapted William Gillette's play *Sherlock Holmes* for his *Mercury Theatre on the Air*. (Gillette had died on 29 April 1937.) Welles was racing through a selection of the more colourful classics of literature and theatre, and this was the twelfth in a weekly series of one-hour broadcasts (the celebrated adaptation of *The War of the Worlds* came a little later). Welles skilfully condensed the play but undertook to play Holmes himself. Neither his voice nor his delivery was anywhere near appropriate: his affected accent made Holmes sound like a conceited dandy, and he gave the lines his characteristically idiosyncratic delivery, rushing phrases and leaving odd pauses. Ray Collins's Watson sounded awful too, but Eustace Wyatt's Moriarty had bite. (It has always been fairly easy to cast a master villain, and Welles himself made an effective job of Moriarty in a British radio adaptation of *The Final Problem* heard in 1954.) Welles's introduction, however, was warmly appreciative of Gillette and Holmesian legend.

But it required no rising star to breathe new life into the master detective. The job was about to be done by a well-known screen character actor, who quickly supplanted Gillette to create *the* Sherlock Holmes of popular memory . . .

BASIL RATHBONE AS SHERLOCK HOLMES

Why was Basil Rathbone so perfect a choice to play Sherlock Holmes? Undoubtedly he was tall and thin, and not far removed from the Paget depictions, yet he had almost invariably been cast as a leading screen villain, memorable from such films as *Captain Blood* and *The Adventures of Robin Hood*. In fact it was his screen image as a villain that helped make him ideal casting for Sherlock Holmes. For the most intelligent and intellectual figures in classic Hollywood films were the villains, who provoked the more "ordinary" heroes into action. And so Rathbone was instantly believable as the thoughtful, calculating Holmes. He also retrieved the part from elderly actors like Wontner and Eille Norwood and gave Holmes back his vigour and some relative youthfulness. And 20th Century-Fox returned the sleuth to a Victorian period setting instead of the contemporary one of all earlier films.

Basil Rathbone (1892–1967) was never more popular than when playing Sherlock Holmes. For many, he is *the* Sherlock Holmes (right). In one of Sidney Paget's illustrations for *The Adventure of the Naval Treaty* in the *Strand* in 1893 (above), the detective, seen conducting a chemical investigation that will determine a man's fate, bears a strong resemblance to Rathbone.

Nigel Bruce made an endearing if often inept Dr Watson opposite Basil Rathbone on screen. This is the duo in pensive mood from *The Adventures of Sherlock Holmes* (1939).

The pair find the body of the convict Selden on the moors in *The Hound of the Baskervilles* (1939).

Fox's 1939 version of *The Hound of the Baskervilles* was faithful to the spirit of Conan Doyle's novel, although it was filmed entirely at the Hollywood studio and its Dartmoor had a cramped, claustrophobic atmosphere. It was excellently cast, even if Nigel Bruce made a somewhat foolish Watson (but not the buffoon of later films), and there was a brilliant stroke in making Lionel Atwill a sinister-looking, older Doctor Mortimer, while the now-forgotten Morton Lowry was exactly right as Stapleton, the daring villain. Stapleton's "sister" really is his sister here rather than his wife, and one who has no part in his schemes so that the romance between her and Richard Greene's threatened Sir Henry Baskerville is unhindered. This change does, however, leave no explanation for the warning note that Sir Henry receives in London, which, in the original story, Mrs Stapleton sent as a reluctant participant in her husband's plot.

No superlative omitted: how Hollywood sold *The Hound of the Baskervilles* to American audiences in 1939. Note the use of Frederic Dorr Steele's drawing of Holmes and Watson finding the convict's body as background material, and also the subordination in the credits of Rathbone and Bruce to the romantic leads.

Even though Conan Doyle refrained from associating Holmes with spiritualism, Ernest Pascal's screenplay added a seance (but without Holmes). After Sir Henry's close call with the deadly hound and Holmes's own descent into the dog's pit (a dramatic addition), the film closes with Holmes retiring for the night, uttering the words "Watson, the needle – quick!" as the image fades into the end titles. It is quite astonishing to find a reference to Holmes's cocaine habit in this Code-conscious period of Hollywood film-making, no matter how fleeting. It isn't even taken from the original story, for Conan Doyle had discarded Holmes's drug addiction by that time and concluded events with Holmes and Watson back in London about to relax at an opera. The idea must have been suggested by Holmes's reaching for the cocaine bottle at the end of the earlier *The Sign of Four*, where he seeks to relieve the onset of tedium. However, he hardly needed the stimulation of cocaine after his exertions on the moors.

Rathbone enjoyed playing Holmes: "It was in this picture that I had the stimulating experience of creating, within my own limited framework, a character that has intrigued me as much as any I have ever played." In a contemporary review of the film, Graham Greene regretted the film's emphasis on action and criticized Rathbone's work: "What is wrong, surely, is Mr Rathbone's reading of the great character: the good humour (Holmes very rarely laughed) and the general air of brisk good health."

Rathbone did give Holmes more warmth and charm than Conan Doyle had intended, and in this and subsequent films he provided what has become popularly accepted as the definitive representation of Holmes, against which others are judged. From the continuing popularity of the Rathbone pictures, it is evident that this is the kind of Holmes that audiences liked and preferred. According to British film expert and television buyer Leslie Halliwell: "statistics show that throughout the world it is the most popular series of films ever televised, and the prediction is that it will go on running until the negatives wear out." But it is interesting to find Rathbone writing in his autobiography: "towards the end of my life with him I came to the conclusion that there was nothing lovable about Holmes."

Fox made only one further Holmes picture with Rathbone, *The Adventures of Sherlock Holmes*, which was suggested by the company's 1932 film with Clive Brook. Both films begin with Moriarty in court and have him plotting to discredit and ruin Holmes. Here "the evil Genius of Crime" (as the foreword describes him) is acquitted for lack of evidence, and Holmes bursts into the courtroom with new proof of his guilt just a fraction too late. (It is odd that Conan Doyle never mentioned Holmes at a trial, and this is perhaps the only time that Holmes has been shown in a courtroom. In the 1932 film, he was absent when the convicted Moriarty issued his threats from the dock.)

This time Holmes and Moriarty have their talk in a shared hansom cab. George Zucco, in beard and thick glasses, makes an impressively cool and confident Moriarty, who is, in Graham Greene's felicitous phrase, "viciously correct". He levels with Holmes: "The situation has become impossible . . . I'm going to break you, Holmes. I'm going to bring off right under your nose the most incredible crime of the century and you'll never suspect it until it's too late. That'll be the end of you, Mr. Holmes." Here, it is Moriarty who looks forward to retirement, so that he can pursue abstract science. Holmes expresses his respect: "I hold you in the highest esteem – but only as a knave."

Moriarty plans to steal the Crown Jewels and distracts Holmes with a murder designed to intrigue him. A club-footed South American with a bolas is the killer whose eerie flute-playing is heard in advance of his crimes. Holmes masquerades as a song-and-dance man at a party (a very convincing disguise and the best remembered of many in the Rathbone films). When a clean-shaven Moriarty turns up at the Tower of London as a sergeant leading a phoney bunch of policemen, the film begins to resemble the broad comedy of Will Hay's contemporary *Where's That*

The artists who originally illustrated Conan Doyle's stories never bothered to depict Mrs Hudson, but here is Mary Gordon as the matronly landlady in *The Adventures of Sherlock Holmes* (1939).

Fire? with its phoney firemen invading the Tower after the same treasure. Holmes and Moriarty wrestle on the high battlements, and Moriarty plunges to his death through an embrasure (only to bounce back, of course, in later films). Before this weak climax, *The Adventures of Sherlock Holmes* delights with its evocation of a foggy, gaslit London of hansom cabs rattling along cobbled streets past leafy squares: like *The Hound of the Baskervilles*, it was a beautifully mounted example of the Hollywood studio system at its best.

Although Fox later continued this vein of Victorian melodrama with such fine films as *The Lodger* and *Hangover Square*, the company dropped Sherlock Holmes. Rathbone and Bruce were signed to star in a half-hour radio series called *Sherlock Holmes*, with scripts once again by Edith Meiser, and did five seasons together until 1946, after which Nigel Bruce partnered Tom Conway for a season.

In March 1942, Universal acquired film rights to all the short stories (but none of the novels) from the Conan Doyle estate, paying $36,000 a year to film up to three stories plus one original story annually, with options that could be extended up to 21 years. Universal made 12 films for release from 1942 to 1946, all but the first directed by Roy William Neill. All the films were updated to the then present time, although inappropriate sets conveyed a quaint, unreal image of British life, and none of them bore more than a slight resemblance to Conan Doyle's plots, although several were falsely stated to be derived from specific stories, perhaps to conform to contractual obligations. Some of the pictures carried a title declaring that Holmes "is ageless, invincible and unchanging. In solving significant problems of the present day he remains – as ever – the supreme master of deductive reasoning". However, the films had no pretensions to provide more than easily digested entertainment: they were not concerned with logic but had to be fast-moving and undemanding.

Some Sherlockian addicts are disconcerted by the spectacle of Holmes tracking down Nazis in the first three Universal pictures as well as by his restyled coiffure with locks of side hair swept forward over his temples. Yet it is surely right to see such a quintessentially English character helping the war effort in the tradition established by Sir Arthur in *His Last Bow*.

Production started in May 1942 on the unequivocally named *Sherlock Holmes Saves London*. Later retitled *Sherlock Holmes and the Voice of Terror*, its release was

Here is Basil Rathbone with the ruffled coiffure of his World War II capers, seen with Evelyn Ankers and Nigel Bruce in *Sherlock Holmes and the Voice of Terror* (1942).

delayed several months in Britain, apparently from fears that it would lower morale through its depiction of a successful Nazi terror campaign and a German spy in the British war cabinet. Holmes makes some dazzling deductions, recognizing a variety of clay known only in Sevenoaks on a minister's foot in Whitehall. He also reads the age of a scar that should be more than twenty years old and that betrays the villain who, in what Holmes describes as "a colossal piece of egocentric conceit", invited him to take on the case. Backed by the Prime Minister, who orders the entire cabinet to accompany Holmes, the detective upsets the German invasion plans and exposes the spy network. The credits state that the film is based on *His Last Bow*, but it only directly borrows that tale's concluding speech about "an east wind coming" to provide a patriotically stirring finish.

Sherlock Holmes and the Secret Weapon revived Moriarty (played with relish by Lionel Atwill) as an agent trying to sell a new gunsight to the Germans. Basil Rathbone disguises himself as a bookseller, lascar and foreign scientist in a ding-dong battle with Moriarty that captures the essence of their relationship. "Just like old times – a battle of wits!" exclaims Moriarty, who keeps score with an abacus that has miniature skulls mounted on the rods. When the captive Holmes proposes a slow death for himself to gain time for a rescue, Moriarty is thrilled by his suggestion of draining blood drop by drop, commenting, "The needle to the last!" The Napoleon of Crime is almost sorry at the prospect of losing Holmes – "You were a stimulating influence to me." When last seen, chased by a freed Holmes, he is falling down a sewer.

The film made a rare acknowledgement of Watson as Holmes's biographer, although he seems so childishly foolish in this Universal series that any literary effort would be beyond him. Dennis Hoey was introduced as the series' Lestrade, so unintelligent that his promotion to Inspector is a miracle. The script was allegedly based on *The Dancing Men*, but it borrowed only the idea of a cipher composed of stick men. It ended on a patriotic note with Holmes thoughtfully looking at Watson and quoting Shakespeare's *Richard II*: "this blessed plot, this earth, this realm, this England."

Sherlock Holmes in Washington was an admitted original and rather flavourless, despite the casting of George Zucco as the leader of the spy ring Holmes exposes in the American capital. The opening scenes in London include the Baker Street lodgings, where a recent-looking set of bullet holes spelling out "VR" seem somewhat anachronistic. Zucco, wearing a toupee, was an excellent villain again, not at all fooled by Holmes's masquerade as an eccentric art collector in his antique shop. At the end, as Holmes and Watson are driven past the Capitol dome, Holmes quotes Winston Churchill: "the British and American people will walk together in majesty, in justice and in peace." It is reminiscent of the hands-across-the-sea sentiment expressed by Conan Doyle in *The Noble Bachelor*.

In *Sherlock Holmes Faces Death*, writer Bertram Millhauser (who had scripted the 1932 Fox film and also worked on four other of the Universal films) re-wrote *The Musgrave Ritual*, including the ritual itself, which is now couched in the form of a chess game. Dr Watson, who is working at gloomy, ghost-ridden Musgrave Manor with mentally disturbed army officers, brings in Holmes to investigate what becomes a series of murders. (Holmes is first seen shooting holes in Mrs Hudson's walls at Baker Street, as mentioned in the Conan Doyle story, but here it is not one of his "queer humours" but relates to a current murder case.) The plot development is ingenious, and the film is quite satisfying and worthy of Holmes's participation. Pictorially, it leaned towards horrific melodrama wherever possible. For economy's sake, the village, featuring a pub called The Rat and the Raven, was the one used in *Frankenstein* films, here passed off as somewhere in Northumberland.

Millhauser's screenplay for *Sherlock Holmes and the Spider Woman* was another very acceptable contribution to the series. It created a formidable adversary in Gale Sondergaard's Spider Woman, who almost has Dr Watson unwittingly shoot Holmes when he is tied to a target representing Hitler at a fairground shooting gallery. The film was a veritable anthology of quotes. Millhauser blends elements derived from *The Final Problem* (Holmes's faked death in a raging torrent), *The Empty House* (Watson nearly fainting on Holmes's reappearance in disguise, and a joke about him *not* being an elderly man carrying books), *The Speckled Band* (a poisonous spider sent through a ventilator), *The Devil's Foot* (deadly fumes from a fire) and *The Sign of Four* (the accomplice who leaves "the footprints of a child"), and it even adapted a quote from *The Yellow Face* (Holmes to Watson: "If you ever find me getting too cocksure again . . . just whisper the word 'pygmy'.") Additionally, Watson refers to the famous untold case, *The Giant Rat of Sumatra*.

Besides directing, Roy William Neill co-wrote *The Scarlet Claw*, which was essentially a horror film, set in the backwoods of Canada and largely played at night or in gloomily-lit interiors. The case recalls *The Hound of the Baskervilles*, but Holmes again has no time for supernatural explanations, and an apparition in the marshes proves to be the result of the application of phosphorus as happened to the jaws of the Hound on Dartmoor. In this dark case, Holmes saves only one of a revenge-seeking actor's intended victims, but he adopts the satisfying device of becoming an actor himself to stand in for the last on the killer's list. The film closes with Holmes eulogizing Canada in the words of Winston Churchill.

There was a horrific element to the next film, *The Pearl of Death*, in the form of the grotesquely featured Hoxton Creeper who breaks men's backs; he was played by Rondo Hatton, a real-life victim of acromegaly. Bertram Millhauser skilfully used the basic premise of *The Six Napoleons*, creating a new master of crime, Giles Conover (played by Miles Mander), of whom Holmes can say (as he originally said of Moriarty): "If I could free society of this sinister creature, I should feel my own career had reached its summit." Holmes makes an uncharacteristic slip when he disconnects a museum's alarm system and allows the precious Borgia Pearl to be stolen (thereby temporarily ruining his reputation). But by the end he is confident enough that the pearl is inside the sixth bust of Napoleon to declare, "If it isn't, I shall retire to Sussex and keep bees". (It is, but he does anyway.) As in *The Scarlet*

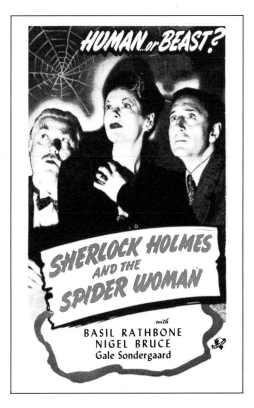

The advertising art casts this film in the horror mould. The studio revived Gale Sondergaard's character for another thriller, *The Spider Woman Strikes Back* (1945), without Holmes.

Having disguised himself as the doctor who is the intended victim of the sadistic jewel thief Giles Conover (Miles Mander), Sherlock Holmes (Rathbone) captures his quarry in *The Pearl of Death* (1944). But Conover soon turns the tables and brings on his ally, the back-breaking Creeper...

Having bagged a huge catch of villains in *The House of Fear* (1945), Basil Rathbone's Sherlock Holmes explains all to Dennis Hoey's Inspector Lestrade, holding the gun. Comrades in custody are played (left to right) by Harry Cording, Paul Cavanagh, Holmes Herbert, Dick Alexander (rear), and Cyril Delevanti.

Claw and the earlier *Secret Weapon*, Holmes disguises himself as the final target of the villain.

The House of Fear was purportedly based on *The Five Orange Pips*. Roy Chanslor's screenplay used the dried pips as a forewarning of death but decreased their number as members of a Scottish club, gathered in a gloomy castle, disappear one by one. The plot was ingenious but had nothing to do with Conan Doyle, and Inspector Lestrade was becoming more stupid than ever, even being ridiculed by Doctor Watson.

For *The Woman in Green*, Bertram Millhauser brought back Moriarty. Investigating the "Finger Murders", in which women victims have their right forefingers expertly severed, Holmes sees signs of "the most brilliant and ruthless intellect the world has ever known". "Steady, Holmes, you've got him on the brain," is Watson's characteristic response. Believed hanged in Montevideo a year before, Moriarty lives to lure Watson away from Baker Street on a false medical errand so that he can interrupt Holmes playing the violin and have the customary few private words based on the famous interview in *The Final Problem*.

Moriarty: "Everything that I have to say to you has already crossed your mind."

Holmes: "And my answer has no doubt crossed yours."

And Moriarty, a little later: "If you *are* instrumental in any way in bringing about my destruction, you will not be alive to enjoy your satisfaction."

The Napoleon of Crime was played by Henry Daniell. Rathbone later said: "There were other Moriartys, but none so delectably dangerous as was that of Henry Daniell." Yet after Ernest Torrence, Lyn Harding, George Zucco and Lionel Atwill, this Moriarty seems rather pallid. Millhauser displays his usual interest in the original stories by working the assassination attempt of *The Empty House* into the narrative, but his climax of a supposedly hypnotized Holmes walking along a high ledge is far-fetched. Moriarty takes the usual death fall.

The series plunged to its lowest point with two scripts by new writers. *Pursuit to Algiers* required Holmes to escort the heir to the throne of a mythical kingdom on a sea voyage. It is particularly galling that when, at long last, Watson decides that the world is sufficiently prepared to hear the story of the Giant Rat of Sumatra and starts relating it to his fellow passengers, the camera cuts away to continue *this* dreary tale! At least Rex Evans's villain has such respect for Holmes that he apologizes in advance of attempting to kill him, and it is good to see Morton Lowry, the excellent Stapleton of the 1939 *Hound of the Baskervilles*, in a key role. The second film, *Terror by Night*, depicts Holmes guarding a precious jewel on the London-to-Edinburgh express train in the hope that Colonel Sebastian Moran will attempt to steal it. Alan Mowbray's appearance as Moran, with a nasty dart-firing air pistol, is the only highlight on a tedious journey.

But when the writers of these two let-downs, Leonard Lee and Frank Gruber, combined efforts for *Dressed to Kill* (in Britain, *Sherlock Holmes and the Secret Code*), the result was most interestingly keyed to the original stories. Here for once in the series was a thoughtful Holmes, worrying all night over the code hidden in the musical variations in the tune of some musical boxes. Here, too, is a more sensible Watson as the chronicler of Holmes's adventures, with *A Scandal in Bohemia* in the current issue of *The Strand Magazine*, and Holmes asking for less emphasis on the melodramatic and more on the intellectual issues of his work. Here, too, is a beautiful schemer who uses the public knowledge of Sherlock Holmes. She lures him into a trap by leaving a tell-tale cigarette knowing of his published study of 140 varieties of cigarette ash, and she uses Holmes's method, described in the newly published story, to fool Watson with a smoke bomb into betraying the whereabouts of a vital musical box. She even adopts a disguise that fools Holmes as did Irene Adler. One feels that Holmes should have replaced the hidden engraving plates in the bookcase with a personal message when he traps her in the act of removing them. She praises him as far cleverer than she had anticipated and Holmes replies: "I shall always cherish the memory of your flattering words." There is, properly, no suggestion that she has overtaken Irene Adler in Holmes's regard. Patricia Morison is most effective playing this dangerous female, called Hilda Courtney.

It is insulting to suggest that Rathbone ever looked bored or disinterested in playing the screen Holmes. He was far too well-trained and professional an actor for that. But, like Conan Doyle before him, and like William Gillette at times, he felt trapped by Sherlock Holmes. The detective had a habit of overwhelming those too closely associated with him. For Rathbone:

the continuous repetition of story after story left me virtually repeating myself each time in a character I had already conceived and developed. The stories varied but I was always the same character merely repeating myself in different situations. . . . I had had seven years of Sherlock Holmes and was not only tired and bored with the series, but felt myself losing ground in other fields of endeavour. And last but not least I was literally aching to get back to my first love, the theatre.

He was plagued by school children who wanted the autograph of Sherlock Holmes and didn't know his real name, "Hi there, Sherlock, how's Doctor Watson?" was the way he sardonically entitled one of the chapters of his autobiography, *In and Out of Character*.

Rathbone had also been heard in 213 half-hour radio broadcasts with Nigel Bruce, the last on 27 May 1946 (*The Singular Affair of the Baconian Cipher*). He was offered a seven-year contract to continue but refused and went off to New York. After Tom Conway had replaced him for one season, John Stanley followed for two seasons, one with Nigel Bruce and one with a new Watson, Alfred Shirley. Then a new team of Ben Wright and Eric Snowden took over for a final American radio series in 1949–50.

It looked as though public interest in Sherlock Holmes was nearing exhaustion. Of course, the original stories were still selling and there was even a collection of the best pastiches (33 in all) issued in 1944 as *The Misadventures of Sherlock Holmes* under the editorship of Ellery Queen. There was a stir when Robert A. Cutter wrote *The Adventure of the Tall Man* from a genuine outline by Sir Arthur Conan Doyle, but as the original author had not considered it worth developing further, it is not surprising that the story (published in 1947) has been largely forgotten.

Then in 1948 there appeared *The Case of the Man Who Was Wanted* (*Cosmopolitan*, August issue), which seemed to be an unpublished Conan Doyle work. It later transpired, however, that the story belonged to an Arthur Whitaker who had sent it to Conan Doyle in 1910, asking him to collaborate. Whitaker had ultimately sold the rights to the plot for £10 to Conan Doyle for the latter's own later use if required.

But when *The Strand Magazine* published an obituary of Holmes by E.V. Knox in the December 1948 issue, it seemed at last as though the bell tolled for the master sleuth. And when the *Strand* itself folded after the March 1950 issue, it seemed the end of an era. Even when Basil Rathbone – again like Conan Doyle and William Gillette – found that he couldn't resist the temptation to revive Holmes, this time in the rising medium of television, the result was a failure. The live show, a pilot for a series, led nowhere. On both sides of the Atlantic, the great detective seemed to have had his day.

10 HOLMES IN ECLIPSE

In 1951, post-war optimism brought about the Festival of Britain. As part of the celebrations, the Borough of Marylebone paid tribute to its "most distinguished resident" by mounting an exhibition at Abbey House, the headquarters of the Abbey National Building Society, which includes 221B Baker Street. Letters to *The Times* from Doctor Watson, Mycroft Holmes, Mrs Hudson and even Inspector Lestrade encouraged the local authority to proceed with its plans.

For the 54,000 visitors who paid their one shilling (5p) admission, the highlight of the exhibition was the reconstruction of the great man's consulting-cum-sitting room (created by stage designer Michael Weight). The thoroughly convincin display helped spread the notion that Sherlock Holmes was a real person – or so tl. stories go. One reporter is said to have asked which of the exhibits had actually belonged to Sherlock Holmes. One visitor is recorded as having remarked, "How very interesting! My son went to school with him", and another to have wondered, "What will he say when he comes back?"

The exhibition ran from 21 May to 22 September 1951, then opened in New York City on 2 July 1952 before moving to Toronto. On 12 December 1957, a large part of the specially created room was fitted into first-floor space at the Sherlock Holmes Public House and Restaurant in Northumberland Street, near Charing Cross – the location of the Northumberland Hotel where Sir Henry Baskerville stayed and had his boots stolen. The room remains there to this day, together with a fine range of wall exhibits, a mecca for all Holmes enthusiasts visiting London.

The sitting room at 221B Baker Street as constructed for the 1951 exhibition. The bust which drew Colonel Moran's fire in *The Empty House* is conspicuous at the window near the "chemical corner". Unanswered correspondence is skewered to the mantelpiece and the Persian slipper containing Holmes's tobacco is hung up by the fire.

The Sherlock Holmes Public House and Restaurant at 10 Northumberland Street near Charing Cross is the former Northumberland Hotel featured in *The Hound of the Baskervilles*. As such it is a highly appropriate location for London's richest concentration of Holmesiana available for public view. There are photographs, drawings and other items arranged throughout the building, while upstairs the Baker Street sitting room has been reconstructed from the 1951 exhibition so that it can be viewed while dining in the restaurant. Note the "VR" scored in bullet holes by the door, the portrait of Irene Adler on the mantelpiece and the violin. (Photographs by John Edwards).

The 1951 exhibition encouraged the formation of a new organization "to pursue knowledge of the public and private lives of Sherlock Holmes and Doctor Watson": The Sherlock Holmes Society of London, which had a foundation meeting on 18 April 1951 and an inaugural gathering on 17 July 1951. Initially with 100 members, it now has over 600, and publishes the bi-annual *Sherlock Holmes Journal*.

The Society fosters an approach to the subject in which Sherlock Holmes actually existed, as did Dr Watson who actually wrote the stories, while Dr Conan Doyle is regarded as the literary agent who arranged for the publication of the memoirs and possibly wrote some of the inferior ones himself. Watson was a careless writer with an abominable memory and even worse handwriting, hence the mistakes and inconsistencies. Besides news and reviews of Holmesian developments, the *Journal* attempts to unravel this tangled skein. Where *was* 221B Baker Street (since the number didn't exist in Holmes's time)? *Which* university did Holmes attend? How many wives did Watson have and how many wounds? The real chronology of the cases is investigated, along with real-life parallels and the real locations of particular adventures. Some of Holmes's solutions have been challenged, notably for *The Musgrave Ritual*, in which it has been suggested that Reginald Musgrave was the real villain and fooled Holmes (Watson would doubtless call this "ineffable twaddle"). Since the doctor often mentions that names, dates and other details have been deliberately changed to avoid embarrassment, there is a ready explanation for most of his so-called errors (quite apart from the boring and retrogressive notion that the slips were made by Conan Doyle, who was often in haste to meet magazine deadlines and working over several decades of time, often somewhat grudgingly, not being too bothered if there were small lapses as long as readers were entertained).★

In the early 1950s, British television began to take an interest in Holmes. Six adventures were transmitted live in adaptations by the noted film critic Miss C.A. Lejeune. Alan Wheatley played Holmes and Raymond Francis was Watson in the stories, which were not updated but left in period. The Birmingham Repertory Theatre revived William Gillette's *Sherlock Holmes*, perhaps its first performance in 20 years, with Alfred Burke as Holmes, Paul Daneman as Watson and Alan Bridges as Moriarty.

Basil Rathbone was invited to star in an American revival, but he thought that Gillette's work would be "so ludicrously funny today" that he refused. He did, however, encourage his wife Ouida, who had already written one play for him, to turn some of the Conan Doyle stories into a new play called *Sherlock Holmes*, which kept to the original written dialogue as much as possible. While his wife was at work on this project, Rathbone appeared in a live American television adaptation of a new Sherlock Holmes story, *The Adventure of the Black Baronet*, by Adrian Conan Doyle and John Dickson Carr, which was one of a series later published in book form, based on cases referred to by Dr Watson. This particular story concerned "the unfortunate Madame Montpensier", who was mentioned in *The Hound of the Baskervilles*.

Ouida Rathbone decided to use primarily *The Bruce-Partington Plans* and add elements from *The Second Stain*, *A Scandal in Bohemia* and *The Final Problem*. It seems as though she was over-faithful to the source material, for the play was too complicated and dated to appeal to general audiences. Also, for once, Rathbone seems to have been off-key. *Variety*'s critic at the Boston try-out said: "He's nervous, insecure and entirely too animated in the part to suggest the detached and cerebral qualities associated with the master detective." In addition, the show had

★ At the time of writing (January 1986), details of the Society are available from its Honorary Secretary, Captain W.R. Michell R.N. (ret), The Old Crown Inn, Lopen, Somerset TA13 5JX, England.

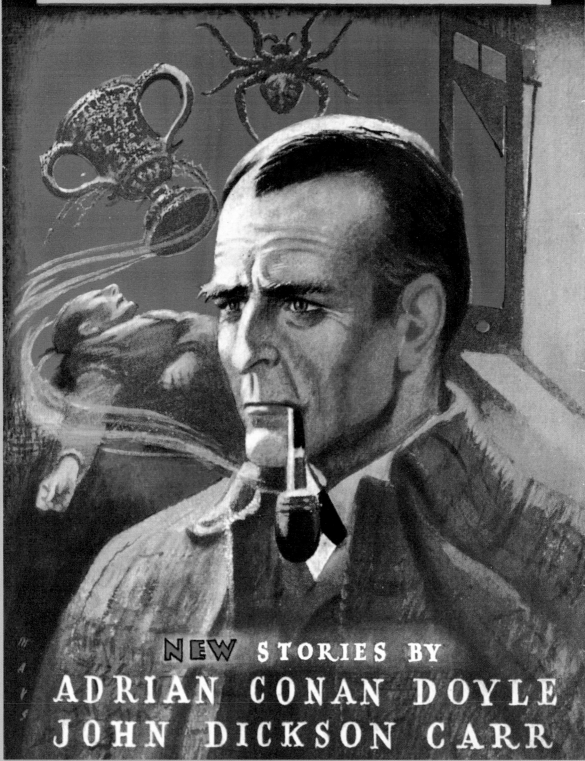

THE EXPLOITS OF SHERLOCK HOLMES

NEW STORIES BY

ADRIAN CONAN DOYLE
JOHN DICKSON CARR

A rehearsal photograph from the short-lived 1953 Broadway production of *Sherlock Holmes*, with Basil Rathbone returning to the part of the master sleuth. Thomas Gomez is a swarthy Moriarty, and Jarmila Novotna is Irene Adler.

too many players and too much elaborate and expensive scenery (including a set of the Reichenbach Falls) to have much chance of recovering its costs.

Rathbone still seemed awkward and ill-at-ease when the production opened on Broadway on 30 October 1953. Ill-health had kept Nigel Bruce from playing Watson and he had died from a heart attack three weeks earlier. Jack Raine portrayed the doctor while Thomas Gomez was an effective Moriarty (he had played a leading heavy in *Sherlock Holmes and the Voice of Terror*). The play closed after only three performances. In his autobiography, Rathbone conceded: "For myself be it said that, like Conan Doyle at the end of the first *Adventures*, try as I would my heart was not really in it." Few youngsters had attended the show, and he concluded that Sherlock Holmes was hopelessly outdated.

The insatiable appetite of American television was responsible for a series of 39 films, each 27 minutes long, made in French studios in 1954. They starred Ronald Howard as a lightweight Holmes and Howard Marion Crawford as a staunch and dependable Watson. Virtually all the shows were original stories, merely using the famous characters created by Conan Doyle.

Opposite, a vigorous representation by D. L. Mays of the great detective with the bushy eyebrows described in *The Valley of Fear* for the British dust jacket of the 1954 collection of pastiches written by Sir Arthur's son Adrian and by one of his biographers, the distinguished crime novelist John Dickson Carr.

The voices of Holmes and Watson on British radio: Carleton Hobbs and Norman Shelley.

Christopher Lee as Holmes with Thorley Walters as Watson in an English pub in the 1962 German production, known in its English dubbed version as *Sherlock Holmes and the Necklace of Death*.

On BBC radio in 1954, a dozen *Adventures of Sherlock Holmes* employed the celebrated voices of John Gielgud as Holmes and Ralph Richardson as Watson, with Orson Welles as Professor Moriarty for the last programme, *The Final Problem*. Carleton Hobbs continued in BBC radio series, but general interest in the great detective had once more fallen to a low ebb.

In 1958 Hammer Films obtained the rights to *The Hound of the Baskervilles*, which it filmed in Technicolor, emphasizing and augmenting the horrific and sensational aspects. A deadly tarantula spider becomes an added threat to Sir Henry Baskerville; a webbed hand is a more graphic link between killer and victim than a mere portrait resemblance; and the former Mrs Stapleton becomes his young daughter – a dark, sadistic siren from the swamps. It was directed by Terence Fisher and starred Peter Cushing, who had done the recent re-makes of *Frankenstein* and *Dracula* for Hammer. Oddly, the film failed to create a chilling Hound and Peter Cushing was curiously ineffective; although his approach was typically conscientious and careful, he was too identified with his recent horror film roles to slip comfortably into the deerstalker and cape, and in any case he was too mild and short for the part. Andre Morell, however, made a refreshingly sensible and upright Watson.

Christopher Lee was more successful as Sir Henry Baskerville, but he too was soon miscast as Holmes in a West German production, *Sherlock Holmes und das Halsband des Todes*. It was written by Curt Siodmak, a fantasy writer who had once scripted a superior "B" film in Hollywood, *The Mantrap* (1943), starring Henry Stephenson as an 80-year-old Scotland Yard chief, a former protégé of Sherlock Holmes called Sir Humphrey Quilp who successfully investigates an American murder case using deductive methods. In the 1962 German film, Holmes thwarts Professor Moriarty, now a famed archaeologist, as the latter attempts to steal a necklace discovered in an Egyptian tomb. Lee perceptively read Holmes as "a very intolerant, argumentative, difficult man" and tried to play him as such. He was also pleased with the way he looked in the part. Working under Terence Fisher again, he

In the 1959 Hammer film production of *The Hound of the Baskervilles*, Peter Cushing's Sherlock Holmes points out to Andre Morell's Dr Watson a telling detail about the portrait of one of the Baskerville line, and (below) questions Ewen Solon's Stapleton with Francis de Wolff's Dr Mortimer holding the lantern. Christopher Lee played the threatened Sir Henry Baskerville.

spoke his lines in English, but when the film was belatedly released as *Sherlock Holmes and the Deadly Necklace* to American television and British cinemas, Lee and Thorley Walters (playing Watson) had been dubbed by unknown American actors, and the atmosphere was wrecked. No one has argued with Lee's assessment of the film as "a badly edited deplorable hodge-podge of nonsense".

The year 1962 was more notable for the publication of a biography of the detective by American Holmesian William S. Baring-Gould. *Sherlock Holmes of Baker Street* (in Britain, *Sherlock Holmes*) slightly indulges the American desire to associate Holmes more directly with the United States, but is a skilful and gently inventive work, consisting of passages from the canonical adventures with new linking text and presenting Dr Watson in a much stronger light than usual. Many of Baring-Gould's ideas – that Professor Moriarty could have been the childhood tutor of

Douglas Wilmer as Baker Street's most famous figure in two of the stories featured in the well-remembered 1965 BBC television series. Right, he fills his pipe from the Persian slipper as Nigel Stock's Watson points out an item in the paper in *The Illustrious Client*. Below, he relaxes at a concert in *The Red-Headed League*, recalling (bottom) Sidney Paget's depiction of the same moment in the *Strand*'s August 1891 issue. (Photographs by Don Smith).

Holmes; that the detective could have met Irene Adler during the Great Hiatus with the resultant birth of a son; that he could have solved the case of Jack the Ripper – were incorporated or re-explored in later books and films. It is to Baring-Gould that we are also indebted for *The Annotated Sherlock Holmes*, a two-volume collection published in 1967 of all of the stories rearranged in chronological order with a fascinating wealth of comment in accompanying essays and marginal notes.

In 1964, BBC TV included a 50-minute adaptation of *The Speckled Band* in a series called *Detective* which was introduced by Rupert Davies in his familiar guise as Inspector Maigret. Douglas Wilmer and Nigel Stock were so impressive in the roles of Holmes and Watson that they starred in a series of 12 adaptations shown the following year. Wilmer made an interesting comment on how his approach to playing Holmes had changed after he viewed his first attempt:

> I thought my portrait of Holmes was incomplete and in places inaccurate; too smooth, urbane and civilized. I've developed it quite a bit since then, because I've realized that he is a much more primitive person, more savage and ruthless. He was a surprisingly unfashionable individual for a Victorian writer to portray, really – completely unsentimental in a sentimental age.

And so Wilmer's Holmes seemed rather harsh and inconsiderate, no longer the attractive figure of Watson's writings or Rathbone's performances. This approach to a sacred figure, though justified by a close reading of Conan Doyle's characterization without Watson's fond and forgiving framework, was not widely liked nor as respected as it should have been. Nigel Stock's Watson was also played more accurately than by Nigel Bruce; he was a believable biographer of Holmes.

The talents of Broadway producer Alexander H. Cohen and director Harold

Prince were behind a Sherlock Holmes stage musical, *Baker Street*, which opened in New York in February 1965 and enjoyed a respectable nine-month run. It was written by a former television writer, Jerome Coopersmith, with other newcomers to Broadway, Marian Grudeff and Ray Jessel, contributing songs and lyrics. Fritz Weaver's Sherlock Holmes and Inga Swenson's Irene Adler had most to do, developing a relationship that could never fully flower and so disappointed uninformed playgoers. Professor Moriarty (Martin Gabel) eventually appeared, intent on seizing the Crown Jewels. Fritz Weaver talked his songs in the manner pioneered by Rex Harrison's Professor Higgins (Harrison is perhaps one star who

Sherlock in song – in the 1965 Broadway musical, *Baker Street*. Above, Fritz Weaver as the detective with Martin Gabel as Professor Moriarty and Inga Swenson as *the* woman, Irene Adler.

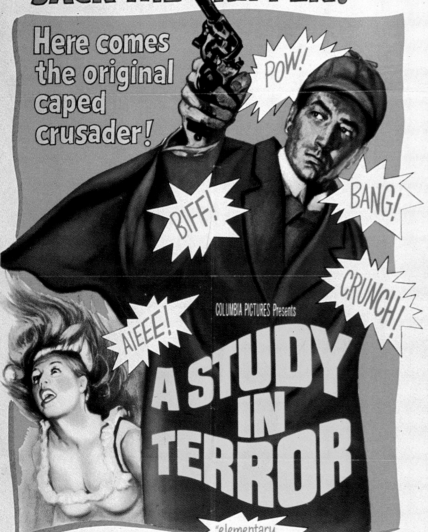

might have played Holmes successfully). Watson had one solo number, "A Married Man". Wiggins and the Baker Street Irregulars performed "Leave It to Us Guv" to some lively choreography. Of the key performance, *Variety*'s critic "Hobe", commented:

> Tall, angular, hatchet-faced Fritz Weaver is a believable Sherlock Holmes. He registers the icy-blooded sleuth's dry impersonality, deductive talent, skill with disguises, knowledge of chemistry and encyclopedic knowledge of odd but miraculously related facts. He also orates a song acceptably, without really singing. He is a good actor who puts across the lines and has reasonable authority. In short, he suffices, without being either brilliant or personally magnetic.

Regrettably, the play never opened in London, nor did MGM (which held the rights) turn it into a film.

The 1965 film *A Study in Terror* initiated a new trend: Sherlock Holmes was no longer interesting enough by himself, but linking him to some other well-known figures of his day, real or fictitious, would intrigue audiences. Here it was Jack the Ripper. Of course, Conan Doyle had never linked Holmes to contemporary figures directly (although informed contemporary readers liked to spot spicy real-life parallels), but Jack the Ripper's activities in the East End had helped *A Study in Scarlet* to success by heightening interest in unsolved murders and detection, and it was quite appropriate that the title should be adapted for use here. Adrian Conan Doyle's Sir Nigel Films (named after the figure in *The White Company* and other of the historical novels) was associated with the production, and there is a huge credit, acknowledging Sir Arthur Conan Doyle's creation of the characters, which dwarfs the story and screenplay credit to Donald and Derek Ford.

Like Hammer's *Hound of the Baskervilles*, the colour production emphasized the horrific elements, and it earned a British "adults only" X certificate; it was primarily sold, and seen, as a horror film. Certainly this is a much nastier world than that of sophisticated criminals like Moriarty, but the story is a convincing, well-developed one with a sound reason for withholding Jack the Ripper's identity at the end (and quite different from that in Baring-Gould's 1962 episode). John Neville is not perfectly cast as Holmes, but Donald Houston is a sturdy Watson. Neville makes an acceptable Holmes after a while and is vocally apt, although he is a bit inclined to rush the displays of deductive reasoning from examining inanimate objects, like a case of surgical instruments. Robert Morley is ideal as Mycroft Holmes, physically rotund just as described in the original stories, and John Fraser, Anthony Quayle, Barry Jones, Judi Dench and Adrienne Corri (in a part possibly suggested by *Veiled Lodger's* Eugenia Ronder) lend distinction to the supporting cast.

The writers worked in many of Sherlock Holmes's best maxims, such as his comment, "You really are an amazing fellow, Watson. Though not in yourself luminous, you are an excellent conductor of light" (from *The Hound of the Baskervilles*), and, although some are awkwardly placed, they brighten up the dialogue considerably. This is a convincing but familiar portrait of the Baker Street duo that only breaks new ground with hints of a politicized Holmes who has condemned prison conditions and has no respect for politicians who allow the poverty of Whitechapel to continue. There is an odd moment at the end of the film when it suddenly abandons its more realistic emphasis. Holmes had seemed trapped in a blazing building and Watson is eager to know how he escaped. There is no explanation other than, "You know my methods, Watson. I am well known to be indestructible." *A Study in Terror* is an interesting picture.

In 1968, the Sherlock Holmes Society of London went on a tour of Switzerland in the footsteps of Sherlock Holmes. Members dressed themselves up as characters from the canon. The Reichenbach Falls were visited, and the struggle between

Opposite, a good film boisterously over-sold by its American distributors to appeal to a young audience addicted to *Batman*. Above, John Neville's Holmes disguises himself as a tramp, eating soup in a poorhouse to gain information leading to Jack the Ripper. Below, Holmes with Donald Houston as his Dr Watson at Baker Street.

A pause in mid-struggle for the press photographers during a re-enactment of the final battle between Holmes and Moriarty by leading members of the Sherlock Holmes Society of London. This took place on 1 May 1968 at the Reichenbach Falls during a "Tour of Switzerland in the Footsteps of Sherlock Holmes" made by the Society's members who dressed up as various characters from the stories. Sir Paul (later Lord) Gore-Booth was Holmes and Charles Scholefield was the Napoleon of Crime. Guard rails now help visitors avoid Moriarty's watery fate. A plaque commemorating Holmes's vanquishing of his foe on 4 May 1891 has been erected in the town of Meiringen. A repeat of the 1968 tour is scheduled by the British society for 1987.

Holmes and Moriarty was re-enacted; there was a debate at Lausanne University on "How much did Sherlock Holmes contribute to modern criminology?"; and there was a visit to the Château de Lucens where Adrian Conan Doyle had established a Sherlock Holmes Museum with a new reconstruction of 221B Baker Street's sitting rooms. The event was covered by 278 journalists, who greatly outnumbered the participants! To the delight of Sherlockians and the Swiss National Tourist Office, the week-long visit became a world media event.

Also in 1968, BBC TV, still in the black and white era, presented a new series of 16 adaptations, but in general they lacked the quality of the Wilmer series (apparently they were made on much shorter schedules). Peter Cushing took over from Douglas Wilmer as Holmes but again proved less than ideally cast, seeming both too old and too energized in the role. Nigel Stock was once more an excellent Watson, and he later starred in a one-man show, *221B*, wandering about a Baker Street sitting room set and relating various of the stories.

The celebrated Hollywood writer-director Billy Wilder had long been a Holmes enthusiast, and he had had the idea of creating a musical long before *Baker Street*. He made two attempts, in 1955 and 1963, to devise a suitable format with lyricist Alan Jay Lerner and composer Frederick Loewe of *My Fair Lady*. He eventually wrote a non-musical script with his usual collaborator, I.A.L. Diamond, and filmed *The Private Life of Sherlock Holmes* in Britain on a huge $10 million budget. He told his biographer Maurice Zolotow:

Peter Cushing succeeded Douglas Wilmer as British television's Sherlock Holmes in a 1968 series. In the adaptation of *The Hound of the Baskervilles*, he gives his parting instructions to Nigel Stock's Watson as the latter departs for Devon.

Right, Cushing's Sherlock Holmes philosophizes about the rose in *The Naval Treaty* ("Our highest assurance of the goodness of Providence seems to me to rest in the flowers"), apparently forgetting the case in hand. (Photographs by Don Smith.)

I wanted to show Holmes as vulnerable, as human. He falls into an emotional dither over a woman and so his mind does not function as well; and actually, you see, in my picture, he does *not* solve the mystery. No, he is deceived. Sherlock Holmes has failed to be Sherlock Holmes precisely because he has fallen in love, and yet he is a better human being that he was ever before.

Holmes in love! Despite Gillette, it still seemed sacrilegious, yet Wilder and Diamond carefully distinguish their Holmes as being the real Holmes rather than the Holmes that Watson described. Here Holmes not only complains at Watson's tendency to over-romanticize, but also that his biographer has exaggerated his height, saddled him with an improbable costume (Watson rightly blames the illustrators for the deerstalker and cape), and exaggerated his skill on the violin and his dependence on drugs.

And this Holmes claims not to dislike women, only to have had bad experiences with them. Although he refuses to answer Watson on this subject, he does relax enough with his attractive client, Madame Valladon (Genevieve Page), when they are masquerading as husband and wife, Mr & Mrs Ashdown, to describe disappointing relationships with at least two women. "The most affectionate woman I ever knew was a murderess: it was one of those passionate affairs at odd hours right in my laboratory and all the time behind my back she was stealing cyanide to sprinkle on her husband's steak-and-kidney pie"; and then there was his fiancée

The British poster for the 1970 film. "Now don't ask me why I'm making a film about Sherlock Holmes," declared Billy Wilder. "The answer is, I love him, and I wanted to."

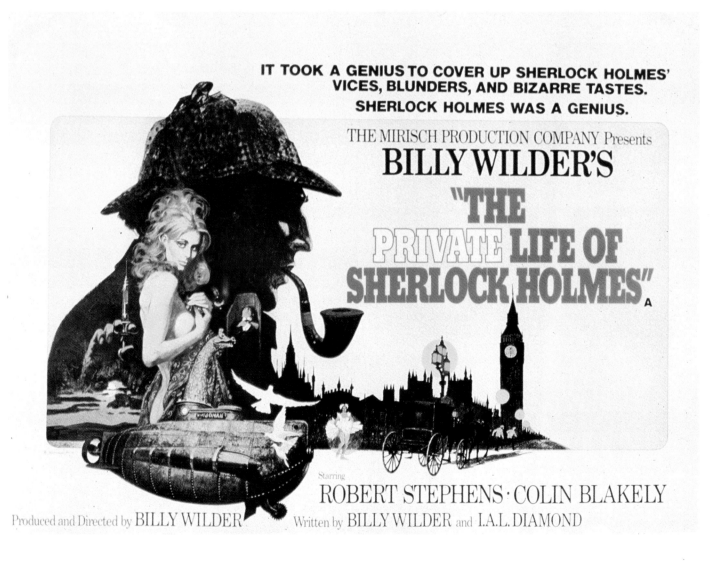

who died of influenza 24 hours before the wedding. For Holmes, these experiences show that "women are unreliable and not to be trusted", and they have left him emotionally crippled.

But Holmes is so taken with the charms of Madame Valladon that he is shattered to learn her true identity as the German spy Ilse Von Hoffmannstahl. He has ignored his brother Mycroft's order to drop his investigation of Monsieur Valladon's disappearance and has exposed a secret submarine base in Scotland to the enemy. But Ilse, who took the assignment because she wanted to "come up against the best", has been affected by Holmes herself, as is shown not only by her facial reaction to being found out but by her later use of the Ashdown name on a mission to Japan.

"We all have our failures – fortunately Watson never writes about mine," this film's Holmes has remarked. (In Conan Doyle's stories, Watson mentions several times that such cases exist, and some of the recorded adventures are partial failures.) Despite the film's title, it must have been disconcerting for cinema audiences to be confronted at such length by one of the great detective's mistakes and to share his emotional discomfort rather than a triumph of deduction. Moreover, the downbeat epilogue was not calculated to please the masses, and nor perhaps did Wilder's ingenious but myth-shattering explanation for the Loch Ness Monster endear him to filmgoers. *The Private Life of Sherlock Holmes* proved to be a box-office disappointment in 1970, but it is one of Wilder's and the cinema's masterpieces. It is the screen's most intelligent, coherent and convincing representation of the detective and his world.

Pretending loss of memory and apparently just fished out of the Thames, Genevieve Page's German spy sets about gaining the sympathy of Holmes (Robert Stephens) in *The Private Life of Sherlock Holmes* (1970).

Above, Sherlock Holmes visits his brother Mycroft (Christopher Lee) at the Diogenes Club with Doctor Watson in *The Private Life of Sherlock Holmes*. Colin Blakely played John H. Watson (right), who was never more a character in his own right than in *The Private Life of Sherlock Holmes*, while in the same film, Robert Stephens (far right) was a commendable addition to the ranks of actors who have played *the* part.

Cast by Wilder because "he looks as if he could be hurt", Robert Stephens has the power and presence to play Holmes well. He has a particular talent for suggesting his petulance and lonely, troubled nature, and a somewhat dissolute look that ties in with this Holmes's dependence on drugs. As played by Colin Blakely, we are given an unfamiliar interpretation of Doctor Watson, but one that is also perfectly believable. Here is a loud, excitable extrovert with normal healthy appetites, for once credible as the man who has "known the women of three continents" (his zest is an important contrast with Holmes's moody aloofness). Irene Handl's Mrs Hudson is a lively character, too, and why not? This isn't quite life at Baker Street as Watson usually described it in his memoirs, but then the biographer wrote in a more reserved and calculated fashion to impress his readers of the time. Though neither corpulent nor lazy, Christopher Lee's smarter brother Mycroft (he anticipates Sherlock at every turn) has an intelligence and asperity that accurately suggests the senior statesman. Besides the casting, the brilliant production design of Alexandre Trauner (a superb reconstruction of Baker Street), the fine cinematography of Christopher Challis, and the affecting bittersweet romantic score by Miklos Rozsa support Wilder's classically relaxed visual style and help to make *The Private Life of Sherlock Holmes* a most satisfying film, especially when seen on the cinema screen in its proper CinemaScope format.

Although it is not evident from the film, it was originally an hour longer and contained several episodes and flashbacks now entirely missing. At present there is only one amusing prefatory episode, inspired by the story of a beautiful woman's proposition to George Bernard Shaw that he should pass on his genius by fathering

Filming of *The Private Life of Sherlock Holmes* on the Baker Street set, 150 yards long, at Pinewood Studios in 1969. The street took four months to build and was designed by French veteran Alexandre Trauner.

These two stills are tantalizing evidence of another of the missing episodes from *The Private Life of Sherlock Holmes* (1970). A blind caretaker named Plimsoll (David Kossoff) introduces Inspector Lestrade (George Benson) to the curious Case of the Upside-Down Room with its dead Chinaman. Apparently, it is a mystery concocted by Watson to try to interest a dejected Sherlock who is contemplating suicide. Although the cut episodes have been cleanly removed from the film, they are said to total as much as 70 minutes, for the film was originally envisaged as a three-hour-plus "roadshow attraction".

her child, to which he replied (as does Holmes), "But suppose, madame, that he should have my looks and your brains?" There was, however, a more elaborate beginning in which Watson's grandson opens the tin dispatch box in the bank vault containing the account of Holmes's involvement with Ilse Von Hoffmannstahl, and a sequence set on a luxury ocean liner in the Mediterranean in which two naked corpses are found in bed and Watson, drunk on champagne, insists on taking charge of the case, leading Holmes to the wrong cabin to disturb two other naked bodies very much alive. There was also a flashback to Holmes's student days at Oxford, rowing for the University team and falling in love for the first time with a girl who turns out to be a prostitute. A further epilogue has Inspector Lestrade asking for assistance in catching Jack the Ripper, but Holmes is too shattered by Ilse's demise to consider it. There has been recent interest among film archives in restoring *The Private Life of Sherlock Holmes* to its full form.

The film takes a few unimportant liberties with details. *The Hound of the Baskervilles*, for instance, is represented as having been written much earlier than it actually was, but that allows the fine joke about the Russian calling it *Big Dog from Baskerville*. What has to be emphasized is that Billy Wilder respected the atmosphere of the stories. He set his account in a nostalgic past, based on papers only released 50 years after Watson's death, and – except in one respect – one can feel that this story might well have happened among all the stories that were fit to be published in the *Strand*. A plot dealing with submarines is fully appropriate, for Conan Doyle touched on the subject in *The Bruce-Partington Plans* and analysed their war-time potential in his fictional short story, *Danger!* (*Strand*, July 1914). The only problem is that there hardly seems room for both Irene Adler and Ilse Von Hoffmannstahl in Holmes's life. They can't both have been *the* woman. In the film, Irene Adler is not mentioned and Holmes's watch, found among Watson's effects, carries Ilse's portrait inside the case.

Another motion picture that failed to spark off any great public enthusiasm was *They Might Be Giants*, the 1971 screen version of a James Goldman play, which had been staged in London 10 years before as a try-out for a Broadway opening that never occurred. In the movie, George C. Scott plays a lawyer widower who has assumed the dress, speech and manner – indeed the identity – of Sherlock Holmes. His acquired acumen enables him to diagnose the problem of another patient at the clinic he attends, and he is equally perceptive in analysing the character of his doctor, Mildred Watson (played by Joanne Woodward), who becomes his willing companion as he travels around New York City in pursuit of an elusive arch-villain: "There are no clues of any kind – it all points to Professor Moriarty." (The unlikely players in the London stage production were Harry H. Corbett and Avis Bunnage.)

The film's title refers to the windmills at which Don Quixote tilted. Though the drama signally fails to reach a satisfactory climax, it has in George C. Scott a most convincing modern Sherlock Holmes in the William Gillette tradition.

They Might Be Giants was released by Universal, which was on firmer ground financially when its television department made a new version of *The Hound of the Baskervilles* with Stewart Granger as Holmes and Bernard Fox as Watson, the pilot for a proposed series of Holmesian adventures. It is of negligible interest, with a cramped soundstage reconstruction of Dartmoor, but it has a good Stapleton in William Shatner; it did not lead to any further adaptations. However, Universal seems to have remembered the premise of *They Might Be Giants* when making the 1976 TV movie *The Return of the World's Greatest Detective*. Larry Hagman portrayed a bumbling Los Angeles motorcycle cop called Sherman Holmes who is concussed in an accident and wakes up believing he is Sherlock Holmes. Aided and abetted by a woman psychiatric social worker, Dr Joan Watson (played by Jenny O'Hara), he investigates the murder of an embezzler. It was by most reports a very average comedy-drama, written by Roland Kibbee and Dean Hargrove.

When an American TV movie was made of *The Hound of the Baskervilles* and shown in 1972, the deerstalker and cape fell on Stewart Granger while Bernard Fox took on the role of Watson.

George C. Scott's Justin Playfair in *They Might Be Giants* (1971) thinks he is Sherlock Holmes and dresses accordingly (left). Scott could have made a magnificent real Holmes. American illustrator Harry C. Edwards's depiction of Holmes at the Reichenbach Falls (for *McClure's Magazine*, December 1893, above) shows him looking amazingly like Scott. The actor did play a Holmesian-style detective in the thriller *The List of Adrian Messenger* (1963) with Kirk Douglas as a Moriarty-like villain and former Sherlock Clive Brook in a supporting role.

11 THE GREAT REVIVAL

In the early 1970s a new wave of interest in Sherlock Holmes was fanned by a theatre production and a best-selling book.

The Royal Shakespeare Company dusted off William Gillette's play for a Christmas 1973 revival at its London base, the Aldwych Theatre. Once again *Sherlock Holmes* was a huge success, later moving to Broadway for further acclamation and a long run followed by a tour. The strength of Frank Dunlop's production was that it treated the play absolutely straight, resisting any tendency to ham it up and play for laughs. The show was great fun, and was enjoyed as thoroughly old-fashioned zesty melodrama on a grand scale. John Wood was a memorable Holmes both in London and in New York, and he was succeeded in America by two former Sherlocks, John Neville and Robert Stephens, and (on tour) by Leonard Nimoy. Doctor Watson was played in London by Tim Piggott-Smith and in the United States by Dennis Cooney and Ronald Bishop. Philip Locke was a demonic Moriarty on two continents, succeeded in America by Clive Revill and Alan Sues. The play has reached even wider audiences in another revival taped for Home Box Office and first televised (in America) in 1981, with Frank Langella, a former screen Dracula, bringing out a romantic irresistibility in Holmes to bolster the love scenes with Laurie Kennedy's Alice Faulkner.

The literary success was Nicholas Meyer's *The Seven-Per-Cent Solution*, published in 1974. It triggered the fashion for "discovering" old, hitherto unpublished and long-mislaid or locked-away reminiscences of Dr John H. Watson (although Billy Wilder's film had been framed in exactly this way). Meyer cunningly provides a story allegedly dictated by Watson in old age that has required "editing" and so may not – it does not – closely resemble his earlier well-known work. In addition, this book, like Billy Wilder's film, purports to show us the *real* Sherlock Holmes while allowing him to apply his deductive powers in the familiar way to a case of major importance. Meyer requires us to accept Watson's admission that he invented his memoirs entitled *The Final Problem* and *The Adventure of the Empty House* to hide the less agreeable truth – that, under the influence of cocaine, Holmes had deluded himself into believing that a humble teacher of mathematics called Moriarty is the Napoleon of Crime, an obsession that is destroying the great detective. Holmes is lured to Vienna, where he is successfully treated by Sigmund Freud. He then helps the psychoanalyst to treat another of his patients and, in the process, uncovers a plot to control a munitions empire. The climax presents Holmes and Freud in tandem as men of action, chasing the villain's hired escape train with a "special" of their own and stripping a carriage to fuel the engine's boiler (like the Marx Brothers at the end of their film comedy, *Go West*). It is gratifying to see Holmes's fencing ability brought into practical use for once as he duels with his principal adversary on top of a moving railway carriage but it is disappointing to be informed that he showed less prowess than his opponent.[*]

The real Sigmund Freud was well acquainted both with cocaine and with Sherlock Holmes through Conan Doyle's stories, which he greatly admired, and Nicholas Meyer cleverly extends the parallels. Both are detectives in their fashion.

The tasteful poster for the 1973 revival of William Gillette's play by the Royal Shakespeare Company, showing John Wood as Sherlock Holmes and Mary Rutherford as Alice Faulkner.

---

[*] It was extraordinarily negligent of the scriptwriters of the Universal series in the 1940s not to have put a sword into the hands of Basil Rathbone, easily the supreme screen fencer of his time.

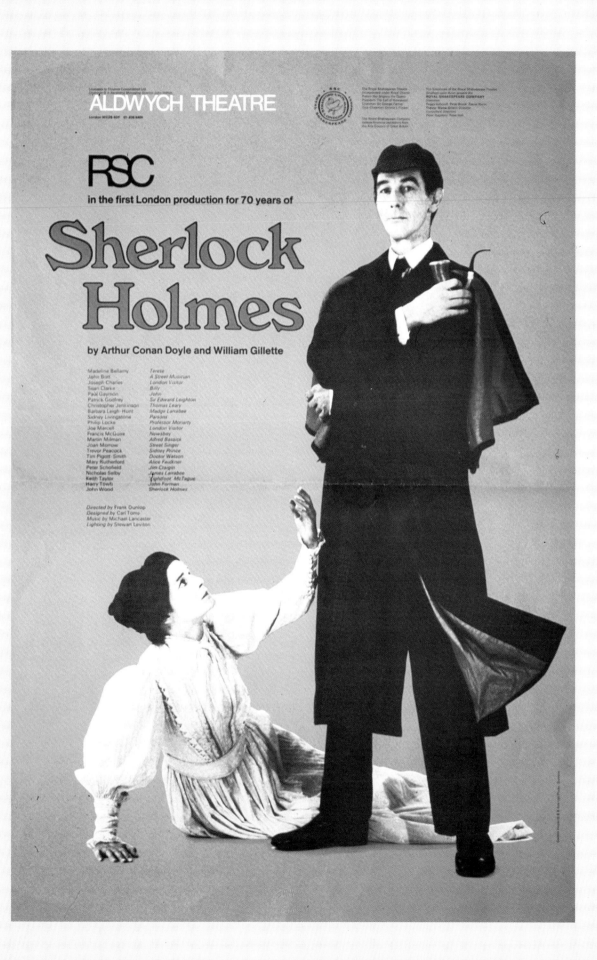

In Meyer's book, Holmes astonishes Freud with the biographical details he deduces by looking around the doctor's consulting room, while Holmes later pays tribute to the Viennese specialist: "You have succeeded in taking my methods – observation and inference – and applied them to the inside of a subject's head." Under hypnosis, Holmes reveals to Freud (and the watching Watson) the dark secret from his childhood that provides the key to his use of cocaine, his hatred for Moriarty and his aversion to women. Watson tells Freud: "You are the greatest detective of them all."

The Seven-Per-Cent Solution offers a more credible account of Holmes's activities during the Great Hiatus than that provided in *The Empty House*. At the end, Holmes goes off alone to find himself, telling Watson that he intends to use the name of Sigerson, not to become a Norwegian explorer but to become a violinist. It remains questionable, however, whether Holmes is well served by being demystified, made a victim of forces beyond his control, a less exceptional person, a *weaker* figure. Most devotees might prefer instead a convincing account of those incredible years of absence exactly as outlined in *The Empty House*.

Nicholas Meyer wrote the screenplay for the 1976 film version of *The Seven-Per-Cent Solution*, which was directed by Herbert Ross. Meyer changed the case concerning Doctor Freud's less celebrated patient into one of abduction of a redhead (Vanessa Redgrave) by the leader of the Ottoman Empire, a genuine enthusiast for scarlet tresses (unlike the organizers of the Red-Headed League). Nicol Williamson and Robert Duvall were unhappily cast as Holmes and Watson, although Alan Arkin made a persuasive Freud and Laurence Olivier was an excellent apologetic Moriarty in his few scenes. Besides being overly drawn-out, the film foolishly prepared its audience for the traumatic revelation about Holmes's childhood by cutting in flashes beforehand.

In his 1976 book, *The West End Horror*, Nicholas Meyer furnished another memoir by Watson. Holmes investigates the murder of an obnoxious critic and blackmailer at the instigation of a penniless rival reviewer, George Bernard Shaw. It evolves into another "big" case with the country's welfare at stake in a rather ghastly way. A surfeit of other famous names from 1895 are part of its tangled skein – Oscar Wilde, Bram Stoker (working furtively on *Dracula*), Ellen Terry and Henry Irving, Gilbert and Sullivan, and Richard D'Oyly Carte. Somehow Holmes pales alongside these celebrities all straining to impress in their brief span of text. They have little to do with the actual case, and there is no convincing explanation for Watson's lapse

In the film version of *The Seven-Per-Cent Solution* (1976), Nicol Williamson (centre in both shots) played Sherlock Holmes with Robert Duvall as Watson and Alan Arkin as the bearded Sigmund Freud.

from his usual practice of disguising famous names (which still allowed them to be recognized by the cognoscenti). There is even room for the wrongful arrest of an astigmatic Parsee and law student, Achmet Singh, a victim of racial prejudice who gratefully describes Holmes as the "breaker of my shackles" when he is released. He combines the characteristics of George Edalji with the vocabulary of Oscar Slater. Intriguing and entertaining as Meyer's two books are, they must be adjudged forgeries rather than convincing Watsonian finds.

Doctor Watson's battered tin dispatch box became a cornucopia for writers. Philip José Farmer edited further papers from it to form his 1974 *The Adventures of the Peerless Peer*, which reveals that Holmes came out of retirement for a second mission against the German spymaster Von Bork, a task that took him to Africa with Watson where they were rescued from a tight spot by none other than Lord Greystoke, Tarzan of the Apes. In Richard Boyer's accomplished *The Giant Rat of Sumatra*, we are finally made privy to Doctor Watson's reminiscences of the case, written in 1912 but withheld until 1974 when the world might be suitably prepared.

And now it could be told, for example, that Holmes collaborated with the American President Theodore Roosevelt six months before Doctor Watson came along (see *The Adventures of the Stalwart Companions*, edited by Paul H. Jeffers, 1978), and that the consulting detective was persuaded to intervene in the Alfred Dreyfus case (Michael Hardwick's *Prisoner of the Devil*, 1979). And then there are Lorin D. Estelman's *Sherlock Holmes vs Dracula* (1979) and *Dr Jekyll and Mr Holmes* (1981), which are much better than they sound. In the latter it is revealed that Holmes solved the Jekyll and Hyde mystery and was the man who shot Doctor Jekyll dead. Holmes then helped Robert Louis Stevenson write the celebrated account of the affair on condition that his own role was eliminated!

Other contemporary figures besides Dr Watson also left accounts that shed new light on Sherlock Holmes, or so we are invited to believe. James Moriarty wrote coded journals of his criminal career, enabling John Gardner to novelize them as *The Return of Moriarty* (1974) and *The Revenge of Moriarty* (1975) and the world to appreciate the Professor's own version of that meeting with Holmes at the Reichenbach Falls and description of his subsequent attempt to wreck Holmes's reputation. Even Mycroft Holmes was industrious enough to leave material for *Enter the Lion* (edited by Michael P. Hodel and Sean M. Wright, 1979) in which Sherlock and he became embroiled in a plot to overthrow the American government and restore the confederacy under British rule. And Dr Petrie, biographer of another renowned crime fighter, Nayland Smith, interestingly records in Cay Van Ash's *Ten Years Beyond Baker Street* a further case in which Holmes was active after *His Last Bow*. Petrie describes how Sherlock Holmes rescued Nayland Smith from his arch-enemy, the fiendish Fu Manchu.

There are many more apocryphal adventures to add to the numerous pastiches of earlier years, which were usually short stories rather than complete books, more closely emulating the Watsonian style. It is interesting that these recent contributions to the Sherlock Holmes saga have shown few signs of lasting power. In Britain in early 1986, both of Nicholas Meyer's books are out of print and only the second of John Gardner's Moriarty novels is still available (in paperback).

It is not only in books and films but also in the theatre that new papers attributed to Dr Watson have been given the limelight. Paul Giovanni's play *The Crucifer of Blood* started life at a small theatre in Buffalo early in 1978 and moved to Broadway. It was later staged in London (Keith Michell playing Holmes), as well as in Los Angeles, where it attracted perhaps the most stellar name to don the deerstalker and Inverness cape in recent years, Charlton Heston. (Opposite him as Watson was the British actor Jeremy Brett.)

The Crucifer of Blood was a re-working of *The Sign of Four*. It followed the example set by Gillette's play and treated a story of a lethal curse as full-blooded melodrama with traditional thunder and lightning. It skilfully incorporated many of

An artist has cleverly merged the familiar profiles of Holmes and Heston to promote Charlton Heston's appearance in a 1980 stage production of *The Crucifer of Blood* at the Ahmanson Theater in Los Angeles.

Christopher Plummer's Sherlock Holmes in the colour production *Murder by Decree* (1979) is a compassionate man truly shocked by the state of one of Jack the Ripper's victims. An equally sober-faced Inspector Lestrade (Frank Finlay) looks on while James Mason's Dr Watson hovers in the background. Right, Holmes locates a key figure in the mystery (Susan Clark) and puts her in danger – here she has almost been run down in the street. He is unable to save her from a ghastly death.

Holmes's celebrated maxims. But it also added a modern twist, the playwright quoting Watson in the programme as having previously spared his readers "the heart of this appalling story" for "no event in my subsequent life could ever erase from my mind the pain and horror" of this "dreadful case". Now at last all can be revealed.... Though ingenious, the new ending does have a belittling effect on Holmes and Watson; it has a cynical, misanthropic thrust that takes away from Conan Doyle's story its positive aspects. Like Meyer's two novels, it shatters the nostalgic charm of the stories by imposing a harsher reality.

There is a similar shaft of dark pessimism behind the film *Murder by Decree* (1979) where only the warm camaraderie of Holmes and Watson (played by Christopher Plummer and James Mason) offers protection from a decadent Victorian world in which the Jack the Ripper murders prove to be deliberate atrocities carried out to protect from scandal the heir presumptive to the British throne. In this chilling portrait of a world in turmoil, the prostitutes are no longer the glamorous figures of *A Study in Terror* but real hags. Holmes finds that he has been used by two factions, even leading the killers to one of their victims. Plummer, who had warmed up for the part by playing Holmes in a British television adaptation of *Silver Blaze*, shown in 1977, gave a fine performance. His is not the great detective as a cold, calculating machine; he is a much more passionate, concerned and sensitive man than we are accustomed to seeing. There is no moment of triumph. Nor can the truth be told.

Although Plummer gave a coherent alternative depiction of Holmes, it is not the authentic Sherlock of Conan Doyle. James Mason brings far more substance and colour than is normal to Watson without enlarging the character out of proportion – for a welcome change, he makes the Doctor an idiosyncratic human being in his own right. The little mealtime incident in which Holmes callously crushes on Watson's plate a pea that has been eluding the good doctor's fork is not only amusing but also evokes the give-and-take of their domestic relationship. Despite some feeble model work of London cityscapes and the use of distorting lenses and zooms that seem anachronistic, *Murder by Decree* is a powerful work, essentially a story of corruption and the abuse of power, only secondarily a Holmes movie.

Like Paul Giovanni, playwright Hugh Leonard (who had adapted Conan Doyle stories for earlier British television series) wrote a play based on supposedly suppressed papers of Dr Watson – withheld because the old boy was under the influence of some of Holmes's drugs! Matters dealt with in *The Mask of Moriarty*, which opened at the Gate Theatre, Dublin, in 1985, were an "impossible" murder on Waterloo Bridge, plastic surgery in the sixth century, the identity of Jack the Ripper and Moriarty's role in making a rare bird extinct. The play was a well-received spoof, with former *Doctor Who* Tom Baker portraying Holmes (as he had in a British television adaptation of *The Hound of the Baskervilles*), but a hoped-for London production did not follow straight on.

Making fun of Sherlock Holmes is difficult, as such writer-performers as Gene Wilder, Peter Cook, Dudley Moore and John Cleese have found. Holmes is so close to being absurd, so much a fantasy figure already, that it needs only the most delicate, slight extension to gain a comic effect, not wholesale exaggeration.

Gene Wilder, who wrote, directed and starred in *The Adventure of Sherlock Holmes' Smarter Brother* (1975), completely overplayed his hand. He had the good sense to cast Douglas Wilmer as Holmes again but then gave him little to do. Sherlock delegates a blackmail case to his younger and (like Mycroft) smarter brother, Sigerson (Sigi), and then pops up at the end to applaud his efforts. Sigi, played by Wilder, is insanely jealous of Sherlock whom he calls "Sheer Luck" (a name that had occurred to burlesque comedians as far back as 1902). His assistant is a sergeant from Scotland Yard, played by the late Marty Feldman and named Orville Sacker; of course, Ormond Sacker had been Conan Doyle's first choice of

Tom Baker (right) as Holmes and Alan Stanford as Watson in the 1985 production *The Mask of Moriarty*, staged at Dublin's Gate Theatre. Baker was no stranger to the part, having starred in a BBC TV production of *The Hound of the Baskervilles* in 1982.

name for John H. Watson. The plot was a re-jigging of *The Second Stain*, working in Moriarty who was enthusiastically performed by Leo McKern. Thorley Walters played Doctor Watson, as he had on television as well as in one of Holmes's more obscure screen appearances (off-screen perhaps) in a lush but little-remembered 1969 comedy *The Best House in London*, in which all kind of celebrities were to be found at a luxurious brothel.

Peter Cook and Dudley Moore, teaming with director Paul Morrissey, made a vulgar send-up of *The Hound of the Baskervilles* (1978), which was greeted with such critical hostility and audience apathy that hardly anyone has seen its absurdities, which included Peter Cook (as Sherlock Holmes) visiting a massage parlour; Dudley Moore (basically playing Watson) in drag as Sherlock's mum at a phoney seance; Roy Kinnear as a female convict on the run (still called Selden); and Baskerville Manor disappearing in a volcanic eruption, a fate that some would wish upon the film. Still, even worse could happen – and did. Sherlock Holmes was starred in gay porno movies.

In one interview John Cleese was quoted as saying of Sherlock Holmes, "I think he was a bit seedy really. A very uninteresting character, which is why we're trying to buck him up a bit." He referred to his work in the dire *The Strange Case of the End of Civilization As We Know It*, shown on British television in 1977, in which he and Arthur Lowe played modern descendants of Holmes and Watson in pursuit of Moriarty's grandson who has threatened to destroy the world in five days. This Holmes thinks he is masterful but he is really a bumbling idiot; this Watson is a cretin who occasionally realizes his stupidity. Cleese, who had earlier attempted to spoof Holmes in *Elementary, My Dear Watson* opposite William Rushton for British TV in 1973, is obviously blinded by being suitably tall and thin into thinking that this perfectly equips him to send up Holmes. In contrast to his *Fawlty Towers*, *End of Civilization* was an hour of turgid slapstick that not even the unusually glamorous Mrs Hudson of Connie Booth could brighten.

There have been new approaches to the character of Dr Watson. In a play called *Sherlock's Last Case*, staged on the London fringe in 1974 (and announced for Broadway in late 1986 with Frank Langella), writer Matthew Lang conceived a Watson so angered by Holmes's cruel treatment of him over the years that he pours acid over the great detective's face. And in a television play, also dating from 1974, Kingsley Amis described a Watson who was more like the rake and womanizer that he claimed to be in *The Sign of Four*. In Amis's *Dr Watson and the Darkwater Hall Mystery*, Watson was played by Edward Fox, an actor who breaks away from the conventional image of the doctor. In Holmes's absence on a rest cure, Watson puts on the deerstalker and cape to look into a case at a Cotswold manor house, investigating the charms of the pretty Spanish maid in bed on the first night!

Not everyone was intent on breaking the mould. Writer Alvin Sapinsley and producer John Cutts, when they made the 1976 film *Sherlock Holmes in New York*, had some success in capturing the traditional spirit of Holmesian adventures, as well as providing American audiences with the happy sight of the Victorian detective at work in their own country.* It is a pity that Roger Moore was cast as Holmes, no matter how much his participation may have enhanced the production's commercial prospects. He has a lightweight, flippant manner that is at odds with the essence of Conan Doyle's character as well as the requirements of this particular story. Although Moore is readily believable as a Holmes who (as described in Baring-Gould's biography) had enjoyed a romantic idyll with Irene Adler 10 years before and given her a son, the actor has little gift for registering Holmes's emotional distress when the lad is kidnapped by Moriarty (and he is helped even less by a

The famous duo in America: Roger Moore and Patrick Macnee in *Sherlock Holmes in New York* (1976).

---

* Alvin Sapinsley also adapted H. F. Heard's novel *A Taste for Honey* for the 1955 Elgin Hour comedy drama *A Sting of Death* on American television. It starred Boris Karloff as a honey fancier and sleuth in a small English country town. Called Mr Mycroft, his real identity is the surprise twist at the end.

With Patrick Macnee and Roger Moore in *Sherlock Holmes in New York* was Charlotte Rampling as Irene Adler, the mother of Sherlock Holmes's son.

surprisingly insipid performance from Charlotte Rampling as Irene).

The film borrows the concept of Fox's 1932 *Sherlock Holmes* and 1939 *Adventures of Sherlock Holmes* in depicting Moriarty seeking to smash Holmes's reputation while committing the crime of the century. The crime here is ingeniously different, as is Moriarty's hold over Holmes. John Huston makes a colourful Napoleon of Crime whose desk boasts the actual Maltese Falcon from Huston's 1941 movie, suggesting a hitherto-untold episode in that statuette's history. There were other in-jokes – a governess called Frau Reichenbach who, in a visual pun, falls over – and, with some delightful casting of veteran Hollywood players, the production was pleasantly rewarding.

A British-made television film, *The Masks of Death* (1984), drew Peter Cushing back to the part of Holmes after 16 years, when he played the maestro once again emerging from retirement in 1913. He investigates three deaths in the East End and then, at the specific request of Ray Milland's Home Secretary ("A grave crisis, Mr Holmes!") turns his attention to the disappearance of a German envoy which threatens to bring about war. (Of course, it is clear from *His Last Bow* that in 1913 Holmes was fully occupied worming his way into Von Bork's spy ring.) There is another lacklustre Irene Adler, this time in the form of Anne Baxter, who has nothing to do with the case. Cushing seemed more at home playing the elderly Holmes, while John Mills was a sprightly Doctor Watson.

A new set of television film adaptations for the international market started in 1981 with Ian Richardson as a more than competent Holmes. But the first two productions, *The Sign of Four* and *The Hound of the Baskervilles*, have a fatally perfunctory feel to them. They did little to suggest that the stories had modern appeal. Sheldon Reynolds, who had made the Ronald Howard television series of the early 1950s in France, now embarked on a new series starring Geoffrey Whitehead and called *Sherlock Holmes and Doctor Watson*. It was shot in Poland of all places. The episodes have apparently been seen in some part of the United States but not (by early 1986) in New York or in the United Kingdom. British viewers had the chance to see a skilful television adaptation by Alexander Baron of *The Hound of the Baskervilles* in four parts in 1982, but it was less than memorable because of casting deficiencies: in particular, neither Tom Baker on this occasion, playing Holmes, nor Terence Rigby as Watson hit the right note.

Geoffrey Whitehead played the maestro of detection in *Sherlock Holmes and Doctor Watson*, a somewhat elusive television series filmed in Poland.

123

The young Sherlock Holmes. Above, Guy Henry in the 1978 British television serial, *Young Sherlock*. Above right, Nicholas Rowe in the title role of *Young Sherlock Holmes* (1985) with Alan Cox (monocled) as John Watson in the laboratory of flying inventor Professor Waxflatter (Nigel Stock, left). Also seen, Elizabeth (Sophie Ward), the professor's daughter, with whom Holmes falls profoundly in love.

Variation and novelty must have seemed a better bet to entice modern audiences. For younger television viewers, there were obvious angles of appeal: the independent adventures of the Baker Street Irregulars in a BBC TV series in 1985, and the youth of Sherlock Holmes, about which the original stories are completely silent. Granada TV's 1982 series, *Young Sherlock*, presented an account by Gerald Frow of the budding detective as a 16-year-old at boarding school who comes home in his parents' absence and finds rum goings-on. Even at that age, Sherlock (played by Guy Henry) is incisive, arrogant and clever, and has the bushy eyebrows that Conan Doyle described.

Nicholas Rowe brings a patrician air to the sleuth in a 1985 big-screen production, *Young Sherlock Holmes*, which describes itself as an "affectionate speculation" and offers an alternative version of Watson's first introduction to Holmes when he joins the same public school. Holmes rapidly deduces the salient details about the tubby, bespectacled boy before him, but unlike the *real* first encounter, he immediately explains how he came to his conclusions. The film was made in England by Steven Spielberg's Amblin Entertainment company and written by Chris Columbus (who provided the same company with *Gremlins*).

Spielberg has been described as the natural successor to Walt Disney, and it is easy to see why from *Young Sherlock Holmes*, with its youthful heroes mixed up with exotic villainy and travelling in a primitive flying machine. Some of the special effects are, however, nasty, and it is difficult to distinguish between the hallucinations and the real action. Columbus makes some good use of fencing and comes up with a plump and young Inspector Lestrade already taking lessons from Sherlock. But his attempt to explain the detective's aloofness towards women is weak: the ending, though painful to Holmes, is not psychologically hurtful enough to explain his later attitude, and the suggestion that he will spend the rest of his life being true to his first great love, looking forward to their reunion in the next world, certainly gives him Conan Doyle's belief in an after-life (which, as previously noted, Conan Doyle never did) but is hard to accord with the rational figure of 221B Baker Street. In any case, the romance between Holmes and Sophie Ward's character is not profoundly enough handled to carry so much weight. *Young Sherlock Holmes* is an entertaining enough romp and Nicholas Rowe (last seen in famous profile, puffing at a Meerschaum, riding off into the future) is sufficiently impressive as

Holmes to make one hope to see him playing the part as Conan Doyle wrote it when he reaches the appropriate age.

The box-office disappointment of *Young Sherlock Holmes* in America suggests that Holmes has too dated an image to appeal to modern audiences on the scale necessary to support a major and expensive production. None of the big-screen Holmes films of the last twenty years have been a huge success. The Walt Disney Company is probably on safer ground with its animated feature, *The Great Mouse Detective*, which is taken from a series of books by Eve Titus that re-tell the saga at rodent level: Basil, the famous Victorian mouse detective, aided by a bumbling assistant called Doctor Dawson, battles the Moriarty-like Ratigan, "the most dangerous rat since the Black Death".★

It is to British television's credit that it has recently presented a series of adaptations that have been remarkably close to the spirit and detail of the original stories. Jeremy Brett's interpretation of Holmes, like that of Douglas Wilmer, makes the great detective into an imperious, rude, almost insufferable figure. This Watson (as played by David Burke in the first two series, called *The Adventures of Sherlock Holmes*), is the sensible, dull biographer who always acts normally. It is

Jeremy Brett as Holmes, David Burke as Watson, and the Baker Street set built in Manchester for the Granada TV series *The Adventures of Sherlock Holmes* (1984 and 1985).

★ There have been other series of children's books, such as those by Brenda Silvers concerning Sherlock Hound and Dr Winston (*The Hound in the Highlands* and others), and Alan Coren's *Arthur and the Great Detective* and sequels about a schoolboy who adventures with the famous twosome.

Holmes who is eccentric, leaping across a sofa to open the door, full of exaggerated mannerisms, while Watson is the calming voice of ordinary reason. Here for once is an untidy Baker Street sitting room with Holmes scooping papers off the floor to avoid giving a bad impression to an important client.

Some of the stories have been revised and extended with generally acceptable results. Charles Gray played Mycroft Holmes in *The Greek Interpreter*, where the character puts rather more of himself into the escapade, participating in a new climax, than one would have expected. Eric Porter's Professor Moriarty is named as the mastermind behind the bank robbery in *The Red-Headed League* to establish him for the succeeding episode of *The Final Problem*, where the Napoleon of Crime is also shown peddling fake masters. There is also a small liberty taken with Conan Doyle's text when Sherlock Holmes actually declares to his unhappy client of *The Norwood Builder* that it really is "most gratifying" to hear of his imminent arrest instead of stopping himself short and merely finding it "most interesting". The change is in keeping with the more ruthless and acid image that Jeremy Brett attaches to Holmes. Here really is a cold, calculating machine unameliorated by Watson's admiring gaze.

With plaques like these on display at the Criterion Brasserie in Piccadilly Circus, it is not difficult to believe in the existence of Holmes and Watson. The upper plaque was unveiled by Fabian of the Yard on the outside wall on 3 January 1953. The lower one was installed to celebrate the centenary of Watson's meeting with Stamford in 1981. In a recent and generally superb restoration of the premises to their full Victorian splendour, the round plaque was discarded as not blending in with the decor but the lower one can be found prominently on display on an inside wall, to the right on entering.

Uncelebrated as yet by the British postal authorities, the Baker Street genius has featured on many stamps (above right). Sometimes he has been part of a series devoted to famous detectives and, as is the case with the Nicaraguan stamp from 1972 in an Interpol tribute, he has usually been honoured with the stamp of highest face value.

All the interpretations of Holmes – from Sidney Paget to Jeremy Brett – have to be judged against the test of the original stories. They are the one fixed point in a changing Holmesian universe. The 60 cases still exert their magic. As that eminent successor sleuth Hercule Poirot remarked of *The Adventures of Sherlock Holmes* in Agatha Christie's *The Clocks* (1963):

It is the author, Sir Arthur Conan Doyle, that I salute. These tales of Sherlock Holmes are in reality far-fetched, full of fallacies and most artificially contrived. But the art of writing – ah, that is entirely different. The pleasure of the language, the creation above all of that magnificent character, Dr Watson. Ah, that was indeed a triumph.

Since 1980, with the ending of British copyright 50 years after Sir Arthur's death, the entire collection of Holmes stories has been widely available in rival editions, giving a new boost to their continued appreciation.

And so Sherlock Holmes lives on, and Doctor Watson too. Plaques remind us of their existence in public places from the Criterion Brasserie to Meiringen near the Reichenbach Falls in Switzerland (but where is the statue Holmes deserves?). It has been crudely estimated that a third of Londoners now believe that Sherlock Holmes was a real person. A thousand letters a year pour into 221B Baker Street where, thanks to the Abbey National Building Society, Sherlock Holmes's private secretary has a desk to answer his mail, telling correspondents that Mr Holmes has retired to the coast but is alive and well and wishes them luck. He cannot be dead, if only because there has been no obituary in *The Times*. The newspaper says that it does not write obituaries of Immortals. In the words of Vincent Starrett, Sherlock Holmes was "a man who never lived and so can never die". The first hundred years are only the beginning.

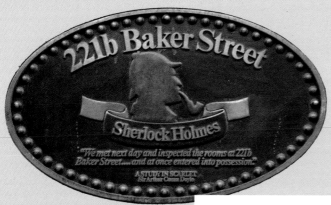

There was no 221B Baker Street when the Sherlock Holmes stories were written. In 1930 a Georgian house, formerly 41 Upper Baker Street, did become 221 Baker Street in a re-numbering scheme but it was demolished that year to make way for Abbey House, which occupies 215 to 229 Baker Street and is the headquarters of the Abbey National Building Society.

The Secretary to Sherlock Holmes,
Abbey National Building Society,
221b Baker Street,
London.

The street views below show the corner with Abbey House today and the same corner back in 1910 (notice how the buildings in the distance beyond Abbey House have survived). By the main entrance to Abbey House will be found the plaque shown above. Right is a selection of the envelopes received, addressed to Holmes or Watson, from all corners of the world – especially America and Japan. Many of the letters contain greetings, but some request Holmes's assistance. All are answered by Holmes's secretary on the notepaper shown.

The Canon

This is a list of the sixty Sherlock Holmes stories by Sir Arthur Conan Doyle in the order they were first published. The four novels are indicated by an asterisk. The dates are those of first publication; in the few cases where the British *Strand Magazine*, was not, judging by cover dates, the first to publish a short story, that journal's date of publication is given also. The anthology in which each short story first appeared in book form is indicated as follows:

[A] *Adventures of Sherlock Holmes*
[C] *The Case Book of Sherlock Holmes*
[HLB] *His Last Bow*
[M] *Memoirs of Sherlock Holmes*
[R] *The Return of Sherlock Holmes*

*A Study in Scarlet
November 1887 *Beeton's Christmas Annual*

*The Sign of Four USA: **The Sign of the Four**
October 1890

A Scandal in Bohemia [A]
July 1891 *Strand*

The Red-Headed League [A]
August 1891 *Strand*

A Case of Identity [A]
September 1891 *Strand*

The Boscombe Valley Mystery [A]
October 1891 *Strand*

The Five Orange Pips [A]
November 1891 *Strand*

The Man with the Twisted Lip [A]
December 1891 *Strand*

The Adventure of the Blue Carbuncle [A]
January 1892 *Strand*

The Adventure of the Speckled Band [A]
February 1892 *Strand*

The Adventure of the Engineer's Thumb [A]
March 1892 *Strand*

The Adventure of the Noble Bachelor [A]
April 1892 *Strand*

The Adventure of the Beryl Coronet [A]
May 1892 *Strand*

The Adventure of the Copper Beeches [A]
June 1892 *Strand*

The Adventure of Silver Blaze [M]
December 1892 *Strand*

The Adventure of the Cardboard Box [HLB]
January 1893 *Strand*

The Adventure of the Yellow Face [M]
February 1893 *Strand*

The Adventure of the Stockbroker's Clerk [M]
March 1893 *Strand*

The Adventure of the "Gloria Scott" [M]
April 1893 *Strand*

The Adventure of the Musgrave Ritual [M]
May 1893 *Strand*

The Adventure of the Reigate Squire;
USA: **The Reigate Puzzle**
[M—as **The Adventure of the Reigate Squires**]
June 1893 *Strand*

The Adventure of the Crooked Man [M]
July 1893 *Strand*

The Adventure of the Resident Patient [M]
August 1893 *Strand*

The Adventure of the Greek Interpreter [M]
September 1893 *Strand*

The Adventure of the Naval Treaty [M]
October and November 1893 *Strand*

The Adventure of the Final Problem [M]
December 1893 *Strand*

*The Hound of the Baskervilles
August 1901–April 1902 *Strand*

The Adventure of the Empty House [R]
26 September 1903 *Collier's*; October 1903 *Strand*

The Adventure of the Norwood Builder [R]
31 October 1903 *Collier's*; November 1903 *Strand*

The Adventure of the Dancing Men [R]
December 1903 *Strand*

The Adventure of the Solitary Cyclist [R]
26 December 1903 *Collier's*; January 1904 *Strand*

The Adventure of the Priory School [R]
30 January 1904 *Collier's*; February 1904 *Strand*

The Adventure of Black Peter [R]
27 February 1904 *Collier's*; March 1904 *Strand*

The Adventure of Charles Augustus Milverton [R]
26 March 1904 *Collier's*; April 1904 *Strand*

The Adventure of the Six Napoleons [R]
30 April 1904 *Collier's*; May 1904 *Strand*

The Adventure of the Three Students [R]
June 1904 *Strand*

The Adventure of the Golden Pince-Nez [R]
July 1904 *Strand*

The Adventure of the Missing Three-Quarter [M]
August 1904 *Strand*

The Adventure of the Abbey Grange [M]
September 1904 *Strand*

The Adventure of the Second Stain [M]
December 1904 *Strand*

A Reminiscence of Mr Sherlock Holmes
[HLB—as **The Adventure of Wisteria Lodge**]
15 August 1908 *Collier's*; September & October 1908 *Strand*

The Adventure of the Bruce-Partington Plans [HLB]
December 1908 *Strand*

The Adventure of the Devil's Foot [HLB]
December 1910 *Strand*

The Adventure of the Red Circle [HLB]
March & April 1911 *Strand*

The Disappearance of Lady Frances Carfax [HLB]
December 1911 *Strand*

The Adventure of the Dying Detective [HLB]
22 November 1913 *Collier's*; December 1913 *Strand*

*The Valley of Fear
September 1914–May 1915 *Strand*

His Last Bow [HLB]
September 1917 *Strand*

The Adventure of the Mazarin Stone [C]
October 1921 *Strand*

In the beginning, there was *Beeton's Christmas Annual* containing the very first Sherlock Holmes story. This is the cover of one of the few surviving copies of the book, a prize item in the Sherlockian collection of Stanley MacKenzie.

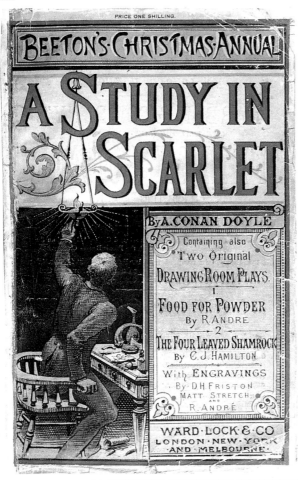

The Problem of Thor Bridge [C]
February & March 1922 *Strand*
The Adventure of the Creeping Man [C]
March 1923 *Strand*
The Adventure of the Sussex Vampire [C]
January 1924 *Strand*
The Adventure of the Three Garridebs [C]
25 October 1924 *Collier's*; January 1925 *Strand*
The Adventure of the Illustrious Client [C]
8 November 1924 *Collier's*; February & March 1925 *Strand*
The Adventure of the Three Gables [C]
18 September 1926 *Liberty*; October 1926 *Strand*
The Adventure of the Blanched Soldier [C]
16 October 1926 *Liberty*; November 1926 *Strand*
The Adventure of the Lion's Mane [C]
27 November 1926 *Liberty*; December 1926 *Strand*
The Adventure of the Retired Colourman [C]
18 December 1926 *Liberty*; January 1927 *Strand*
The Adventure of the Veiled Lodger [C]
22 January 1927 *Liberty*; February 1927 *Strand*
The Adventure of Shoscombe Old Place [C]
5 March 1927 *Liberty*; April 1927 *Strand*

Further Reading

Autobiography of Sir Arthur Conan Doyle

Memories and Adventures, Hodder & Stoughton, London, 1924; Little, Brown & Co., Boston, 1924

Biographies of Sir Arthur Conan Doyle

In order of appearance
Pearson, Hesketh, *Conan Doyle*, Methuen, 1943
Conan Doyle, Adrian, *The True Conan Doyle*, John Murray, London, 1945; Coward-McCann, New York, 1946
Carr, John Dickson, *The Life of Sir Arthur Conan Doyle*, John Murray, London, 1949; Harper & Row, New York, 1949
Nordon, Pierre, *Sir Arthur Conan Doyle – L'Homme et L'Oeuvre*; as *Conan Doyle, A Biography*, Holt, Rinehart & Winston, New York, 1964; John Murray, London, 1966
Higham, Charles, *The Adventures of Conan Doyle*, Hamish Hamilton, London, 1976; W. W. Norton & Co., New York, 1976
Pearsall, Ronald, *Conan Doyle A Biographical Solution*, Weidenfeld & Nicolson, London, 1977; St Martin's Press, New York, 1977
Keating, H.R.F., *Sherlock Holmes: The Man and His World*, Thames & Hudson, London, 1979
Edwards, Owen Dudley, *The Quest for Sherlock Holmes*, Mainstream Publishing, Edinburgh, 1983; Penguin Books, Harmondsworth, Middlesex, 1984

Biographies of Sherlock Holmes

In order of appearance
Baring-Gould, William S., *Sherlock Holmes of Baker Street*, Clarkson N. Potter, New York, 1962; as *Sherlock Holmes*, Rupert Hart-Davis, London, 1962
Harrison, Michael, *I, Sherlock Holmes*, E. P. Dutton, New York, 1977
Hardwick, Michael, *Sherlock Holmes – My Life and Crimes*, Harvill Press, London, 1984

Biographies of Doctor John H. Watson

In order of appearance
Roberts, S. C., *Doctor Watson*, Faber & Faber, London, 1931
Hardwick, Michael, *The Private Life of Dr. Watson – Being the Personal Reminiscences of John H. Watson M.D.*, E. P. Dutton, New York, 1983

A Selection of Literary Studies and Reference Works

In order of appearance
Bell, H. W., *Sherlock Holmes and Dr Watson: The Chronology of Their Adventures*, Constable, London, 1932
Blakeney, T. S., *Sherlock Holmes: Fact or Fiction?*, John Murray, London, 1932
Starrett, Vincent, *The Private Life of Sherlock Holmes*, Macmillan, New York, 1933; Nicholson & Watson, London, 1934
Christ, Jay Finley, *An Irregular Chronology of Sherlock Holmes of Baker Street*, Fanlight Press, Ann Arbor, Michigan, 1947
Brend, Gavin, *My Dear Holmes*, George Allen & Unwin, London, 1951
Roberts, S. C., *Holmes and Watson: A Miscellany*, Oxford University Press, Oxford, 1953
Zeisler, Ernest Bloomfield, *Baker Street Chronology – Commentaries on the Sacred Writings of Dr John H. Watson*, Alexander J. Isaacs, Chicago, 1953
Warrack, Guy, *Sherlock Holmes and Music*, Faber & Faber, London, 1957
Hardwick, Michael and Mollie, *The Sherlock Holmes Companion*, John Murray, London, 1962
Klinefelter, Walter, *Sherlock Holmes in Portrait and Profile*, Syracuse University Press, New York, 1963; Schocken Books, New York, 1975. The illustrations surveyed
Baring-Gould, William S., *The Annotated Sherlock Holmes*, John Murray, London, 1968. The complete stories, arranged in chronological order and liberally annotated
Hall, Trevor H., *Sherlock Holmes: Ten Literary Studies*, St Martin's Press, New York, 1970
Hall, Trevor H., *The Late Mr Sherlock Holmes and Other Literary Studies*, St Martin's Press, New York, 1971
Dakin, D. Martin, *A Sherlockian Commentary*, David & Charles, Newton Abbot, Devon, 1972
McQueen, Ian, *Sherlock Holmes Detected – The Problem of the Long Stories*, David & Charles, Newton Abbot, Devon, 1974
Rosenberg, Samuel, *Naked Is the Best Disguise*, Bobbs-Merrill, New York, 1974
Haining, Peter (editor), *The Sherlock Holmes Scrapbook*, New English Library, London, 1974
De Waal, Ronald, *The World Bibliography of Sherlock Holmes and Dr Watson*, New York Graphic Society, New York, 1974. 6,221 items in 526 large pages
Harrison, Michael (editor), *Beyond Baker Street – A Sherlockian Anthology*, Bobbs-Merrill, New York, 1976
Tracy, Jack, *The Encyclopedia Sherlockiana*, Doubleday & Co. Inc., New York, 1977; Avon Books, New York, 1979
Haining, Peter (editor), *A Sherlock Holmes Compendium*, W.H. Allen, London, 1980

De Waal, Ronald Burt, *The International Sherlock Holmes*, Archon, Connecticut, 1980; Mansell, London, 1980. Index of 6,135 items about Sherlock Holmes, supplementing 1974 compilation
Blackbeard, Bill, *Sherlock Holmes in America*, Harry N. Abrams, New York, 1981. Study of illustrations
Green, Richard Lancelyn and Gibson, John Michael, *A Bibliography of A. Conan Doyle*, Clarendon Press, Oxford, 1983. Fully detailed record of all published works in English
Green, Richard Lancelyn, *The Uncollected Sherlock Holmes*, Penguin Books, Harmondsworth, Middlesex, 1983. Includes Conan Doyle's pastiches, *The Field Bazaar* and *How I Learned the Trick*, also script of Conan Doyle's stage adaptation of *The Speckled Band* (as *The Stonor Case*) and his play *The Crown Diamond*; extracts from *Memories and Adventures* re Sherlock Holmes; and much more
Shreffler, Philip A. (editor), *Baker Street Studies – Cornerstone Writings About Sherlock Holmes*, Greenwood Press, Westport, Connecticut and London, 1984. Includes Ronald A. Knox's classic 1912 paper and Vincent Starrett's poem *221B*
Shepherd, Michael, *Sherlock Holmes and the Case of Dr Freud*, Tavistock Publications, London and New York, 1985

In addition to these, there are, of course, the two magazines *The Sherlock Holmes Journal* and *The Baker Street Journal*, which are invaluable sources of information and theory. The first is obtained by joining The Sherlock Holmes Society of London (see page 101), the second from the address given in the footnote on page 79.

Collections of Short Pastiches

In order of appearance
Queen, Ellery (editor), *The Misadventures of Sherlock Holmes*, Little, Brown & Co., Boston, 1944. 33 pastiches
Conan Doyle, Adrian, and Carr, John Dickson, *The Exploits of Sherlock Holmes*, John Murray, London, 1954; Random House, New York, 1954. 12 pastiches
Green, Richard Lancelyn (editor), *The Further Adventures of Sherlock Holmes*, Penguin Books, Harmondsworth, Middlesex, 1985. 11 pastiches

Sherlock Holmes in Performance

This is a chronological, selective listing of the more important and prominent plays, films, television and radio broadcasts featuring Sherlock Holmes. Dates used are those of first showing, first transmission, opening night, etc., not those of production or try-outs. Characters from the canon who were directly involved with Sherlock Holmes are identified (with the exception of American radio series, which are too numerous to include cast listings, which are, in any case, mostly unavailable). Actresses playing Alice Faulkner in the Gillette stage play are also identified, as are those in a few other roles of special interest. The following abbreviations are used:

sc *script*
adap *adaptation*
dir *director*
prod *producer*

Readers will find many further details (including recordings) up to and including 1974 in *The Public Life of Sherlock Holmes* by Michael Pointer (David & Charles, Newton Abbot, Devon, 1975) and for films only (up to 1976) in *Sherlock Holmes on the Screen* by Robert W. Pohle Jr. and Douglas C. Hart (A. S. Barnes & Co., South Brunswick, New Jersey, 1977). Grateful acknowledgement is made to both these books, although information has been re-researched where practicable. Special efforts have been taken to include more recent works, partly to update the earlier histories and partly because these are more likely to be recalled by readers, even though many in the long term will not deserve to be remembered.

1899

SHERLOCK HOLMES
American stage adaptation
by William Gillette and Arthur Conan Doyle
William Gillette as Sherlock Holmes
Bruce McRae as Doctor Watson
with George Wessells as Moriarty. Opened at Garrick Theater, New York, on 6 November. Opened at Lyceum Theatre, London, on 9 September 1901 with Williame Gillette, Percy Lyndal as Doctor Watson, W. L. Abingdon as Moriarty, Henry McArdle as Billy, Maude Fealy as Alice Faulkner. Various revivals and touring companies.

1905

THE ADVENTURES OF SHERLOCK HOLMES
(Britain: **SHERLOCK HOLMES**)
American film production
sc: Theodor Liebler (from *The Sign of the Four*), dir: J. Stuart Blackton
Maurice Costello as Sherlock Holmes
with Kyrle Bellew, J. Barney Sherry (prod: Vitagraph). Also known as *Held for a Ransom* (Britain: *Held to Ransom*).

1910

THE SPECKLED BAND
British stage adaptation
by Arthur Conan Doyle from his story
H. A. Saintsbury as Sherlock Holmes
Claude King as Doctor Watson
with Lyn Harding as Doctor Grimesby Rylott (not Roylott), Christine Silver as Enid Stonor (=Helen Stoner), Agnes Thomas, A. S. Homewood, Wilton Ross, Arthur Burne, Geoffrey Hill, Frank Ridley as Milverton, Cecil F. Lowrie as Billy. Opened Adelphi Theatre, London, on 4 June.

1912

SHERLOCK HOLMES
British-French series of film adaptations
Georges Treville as Sherlock Holmes
Mr Moyse as Doctor Watson
Eight films made by the Eclair company, directed by Georges Treville, each approximately 1,700 feet.
The Speckled Band (there was no Watson)
Silver Blaze
The Beryl Coronet
The Musgrave Ritual
The Reigate Squires
The Stolen Papers (from *The Naval Treaty*)
The Mystery of Boscombe Vale (from *The Boscombe Valley Mystery*)
The Copper Beeches

1913

SHERLOCK HOLMES SOLVES THE SIGN OF THE FOUR
(Britain: **THE SIGN OF FOUR**)
American film production
Harry Benham as Sherlock Holmes
Thanhouser production. 2 reels.

1914

DER HUND VON BASKERVILLE
German film adaptation
adap: Richard Oswald, dir: Rudolph Meinert
Alwin Neuss as Sherlock Holmes
with Friedrich Kühne as Stapleton, Erwin Fichtner as Henry von Baskerville, Andreas von Horn as Barrymore (Vitascope production). Feature length. Followed by various sequels.

A STUDY IN SCARLET
British film adaptation
adap: Harry Engholm, dir: George Pearson
James Bragington as Sherlock Holmes
with Fred Paul as Jefferson Hope (prod: G. B. Samuelson, distributed by Moss). Feature length.

A STUDY IN SCARLET
American film adaptation
adap: Grace Cunard, dir: Francis Ford
Francis Ford as Sherlock Holmes
Jack Francis as Doctor Watson
Gold Seal (Universal) production. 2 reels.

William Gillette on stage in *Sherlock Holmes*.

1916

SHERLOCK HOLMES
American film adaptation
adap: H. S. Sheldon from the play by William Gillette, dir: Arthur Berthelet
William Gillette as Sherlock Holmes
Edward Fielding as Doctor Watson
with Ernest Maupain as Moriarty, Marjorie Kay as Alice Faulkner, Burford Hampden as Billy, William Postance, Mario Marjeroni, Grace Reals, Hugh Tompson (prod: Essanay). Feature-length.

THE VALLEY OF FEAR
British film adaptation
adap: Harry Engholm, dir: Alexander Butler
H. A. Saintsbury as Sherlock Holmes
Arthur M. Cullin as Doctor Watson
with Booth Conway as Moriarty, Daisy Burrell, Jack Macaulay, Cecil Mannering, Lionel D'Aragon, Bernard Vaughan, Jack Clair (prod: G. B. Samuelson, distributed by Moss). Feature-length.

1921

THE ADVENTURES OF SHERLOCK HOLMES
Series of British film adaptations
Eille Norwood as Sherlock Holmes
Hubert Willis as Doctor Watson
Mme d'Esterre as Mrs Hudson
Fifteen stories usually adapted by William J. Elliott and made by Maurice Elvey for The Stoll Picture Productions; all shorts.
The Dying Detective with Cecil Humphreys as Culverton Smith.
The Devil's Foot with Harvey Braban as Mortimer Tregennis, Hugh Buckler as Doctor Sterndale.
A Case of Identity with Edna Flugrath as Mary Sutherland, Nelson Ramsey as James Windibank, Nessie Blackford as Mrs Windibank.
The Yellow Face with Clifford Heatherly as Grant Munro, Norma Whalley as Effie Munro, Master Robey as the child.
The Red-Headed League with Edward Arundell as Jabez Wilson, H. Townsend as Vincent Spaulding, Arthur Bell as Inspector Lestrade.

The Resident Patient with Arthur Bell as Inspector Lestrade, C. Pitt-Chatham as Doctor Percy Trevelyan, Judd Green as Blessington.

A Scandal in Bohemia with Joan Beverley as Irene Adler, Alfred Drayton as the King of Bohemia, Miles Mander as Godfrey Norton.

The Man with the Twisted Lip with Robert Vallis as Neville St Clair, Paulette del Baye as Mrs St Clair.

The Beryl Coronet with Henry Vibart as Alexander Holder, Molly Adair as Mary, Laurence Anderson as Arthur Holder, Jack Selfridge as Sir George Burnwell.

The Noble Bachelor with Arthur Bell as Inspector Lestrade, Cyril Percival as Lord Robert St Simon, Temple Bell as Hetty Doran, Fred Earle as Francis Hay Moulton.

The Copper Beeches with Madge White as Violet Hunter, Lyell Johnson as Jephro Rucastle, Arthur Bell as Inspector Lestrade.

The Empty House with Sidney Seaward as Colonel Sebastian Moran, Austin Fairman as the Hon. Ronald Adair, Arthur Bell as Inspector Lestrade.

The Tiger of San Pedro (from *Wisteria Lodge*) with George Harrington as John Scott Eccles, Arthur Walcott as Garcia, Lewis Gilbert as Henderson/Murillo, Arthur Bell as Inspector Lestrade.

The Priory School (adap: Charles Barnett) with Leslie English as Doctor Thorneycroft Huxtable, C. H. Croker-King as the Duke of Holdernesse, Cecil Kerr as Wilder, Tom Ronald as Reuben Hayes, Patrick Kay as Lord Saltire.

The Solitary Cyclist with Violet Hewitt as Violet Relph [Smith], R. D. Sylvester as Bob Carruthers, Allan Jeayes as Woodley.

THE CROWN DIAMOND

British stage production
by Sir Arthur Conan Doyle
Dennis Neilson-Terry as Sherlock Holmes
R. V. Taylour as Doctor Watson
with Norman Leyland as Colonel Sebastian Moran, Charles Farrell as Sam Merton, Ronald Hammond as Billy. Opened Coliseum Theatre, London, 16 May. Revised for magazine publication as *The Adventure of the Mazarin Stone*.

THE HOUND OF THE BASKERVILLES

British film adaptation
adap: William J. Elliott, Dorothy Westlake, dir: Maurice Elvey
Eille Norwood as Sherlock Holmes
Hubert Willis as Doctor Watson
Mme d'Esterre as Mrs Hudson
with Catina Campbell as Beryl Stapleton, Rex McDougall as Sir Henry Baskerville, Lewis Gilbert as John Stapleton, Robert English as Doctor Mortimer, Fred Raynham as Barrymore, Miss Walker as Mrs Barrymore, Robert Vallis as Selden (prod: Stoll). Released August.

1922

THE FURTHER ADVENTURES OF SHERLOCK HOLMES

Series of British film adaptations
Eille Norwood as Sherlock Holmes
Hubert Willis as Doctor Watson
Mme d'Esterre as Mrs Hudson
Fifteen stories usually adapted by Patrick L. Mannock and Geoffrey H. Malins and made by George Ridgwell for The Stoll Picture Productions; all shorts.

Charles Augustus Milverton with George Foley as Milverton, Tonie Edgar Bruce as Lady Eva Bracknell, Teddy Arundell as Detective Inspector Hopkins.

The Abbey Grange with Madeleine Seymour as Lady Brackenstall, Lawford Davidson as Sir Eustace Brackenstall, Leslie Stiles as Captain Croker, Teddy Arundell as Detective Inspector Hopkins.

The Norwood Builder with Fred Wright as Jonas Oldacre, Cyril Raymond as John Hector MacFarlane, Teddy Arundell as Detective Inspector Hopkins.

The Reigate Squires with Teddy Arundell as Detective Inspector Hopkins, Richard Atwood as Alec Cunningham, Edward O'Neill as Squire Cunningham, Arthur Lumley as Colonel Hayter.

The Naval Treaty with Jack Hobbs as Percy Phelps, Francis Duguid as Joseph Harrison, Nancy May as Annie Harrison.

The Second Stain with Dorothy Fane as Lady Hilda Trelawney Hope, A. Scott-Gatty as Trelawney Hope, Cecil Ward as Lord Bellinger, Teddy Arundell as Dectective Inspector Hopkins, Wally Bosco as Eduardo Lucas.

The Red Circle with Esme Hubbard as Mrs Warren, Teddy Arundell as Detective Inspector Hopkins, Tom Beaumont as Leverton, Sybil Archdale as Amelia (Emilia) Lucca, Maresco Marescini as Giuseppe Gorgiano, Bertram Burleigh as Gennaro Lucca.

The Six Napoleons with Teddy Arundell as Detective Inspector Hopkins, George Bellamy as Beppo, Jack Raymond as Pietro Venucci, Alice Moffat as Lucretia Venucci.

Black Peter with Teddy Arundell as Detective Inspector Hopkins, Hugh Buckler as Patrick Cairns, Fred Paul as Captain Peter Carey.

The Bruce-Partington Plans with Lewis Gilbert as Mycroft Holmes, Teddy Arundel as Detective Inspector Hopkins, Malcolm Tod as Cadogan West, Ronald Power as Colonel Valentine Walter, Edward Sorley as Hugo Oberstein, Leslie Brittain as Sidney Johnson.

The Stockbroker's Clerk with Olaf Hytten as Hall Pycroft, Aubrey Fitzgerald as Arthur Pinner, George Ridgwell as Beddington.

The Boscombe Valley Mystery with Hal Martin as Charles McCarthy, Ray Raymond as James McCarthy, Fred Raynham as John Turner, Thelma Murray as Alice Turner, Teddy Arundell as Detective Inspector Hopkins.

The Musgrave Ritual (adap: George Ridgwell) with Clifton Boyne as Brunton, Betty Chester as Rachel Howells, Geoffrey Wilmer as Reginald Musgrave.

The Golden Pince-Nez with Teddy Arundell as Detective Inspector Hopkins, Norma Whalley as Mrs Anna Coram, Cecil Morton York as Professor Coram.

The Greek Interpreter with Cecil Dane as Mr Melas, Robert Vallis as Wilson Kemp, J. R. Tozer as Harold Latimer, L. Andre as Paul Kratides, Edith Saville as Sophy Katrides, H. Wheeler as Detective Inspector Hopkins.

SHERLOCK HOLMES

(Britain: **MORIARTY**)
American film adaptation
adap: Marion Fairfax, Earle Browne from the play by William Gillette, dir: Albert Parker
John Barrymore as Sherlock Holmes
Roland Young as Doctor Watson
with Carol Dempster as Alice Faulkner, Gustav von Seyffertitz as Moriarty, Louis Wolheim, Peter Knight, William Powell, Hedda Hopper, Peggy Bayfield, Margaret Kemp, Anders Randolf, Robert Schable, Reginald Denny, David Torrence, Robert Fischer, Lumsden Hare, Jerry Devine as Billy, John Willard as Inspector Gregson (prod: F. J. Godsol for Goldwyn Pictures). 9 reels. Opened 1 May.

Ellie Norwood as Holmes in *The Man with the Twisted Lip*, *A Case of Identity* and *The Beryl Coronet*.

1923

THE LAST ADVENTURES OF SHERLOCK HOLMES
Series of British film adaptations
Eille Norwood as Sherlock Holmes
Hubert Willis as Doctor Watson
Mme d'Esterre as Mrs Hudson
Fifteen stories usually adapted by Geoffrey H. Malins and P. L. Mannock (but many uncredited) and made by George Ridgwell for The Stoll Picture Productions; all shorts.
Silver Blaze with Knighton Small as Colonel Ross, Sam Marsh as Straker, Norma Whalley as Mrs Straker, Sam Austin as Silas Brown, Tom Beaumont as Inspector Gregory.
The Speckled Band with Lewis Gilbert as Doctor Grimesby Roylott, Cynthia Murtagh as Helen Stoner.
The "Gloria Scott" with Reginald Fox as Victor Trevor, Fred Raynham as James Trevor, E. Shannon as Evans, Laurie Leslie as Hudson, Ray Raymond as Prendergast.
The Blue Carbuncle with Douglas Payne as Peterson, Gordon Hopkirk as Ryder, Sebastian Smith as Henry Baker, Mary Mackintosh as Mrs Oakshott.
The Engineer's Thumb with Bertram Burleigh as Hatherley, Henry Latimer as Colonel Lysander Stark, Tom Beaumont as Inspector Gregory.
His Last Bow with Nelson Ramsay as Carl Von Bork, R. Van Courtland as Baron von Herling, Kate Gurney as Martha, Tom Beaumont as Inspector Gregory.
The Cardboard Box with Tom Beaumont as Inspector Lestrade, Maud Wulff as Miss Cushing, Hilda Anthony as Mary Browner, Johnny Butt as James Browner, Eric Lugg as Alec Fairbairn.
The Disappearance of Lady Frances Carfax (adap: George Ridgwell) with Evelyn Cecil as Lady Frances Carfax, David Hawthorne as Hon. Philip Green, Cecil Morton York as Holy Peters, Madge Tree as Mrs Peters, Tom Beaumont as Inspector Gregory.
The Three Students with William Lugg as Hilton Soames, A. Harding Steerman as Bannister, L. Verne as Gilchrist.
The Missing Three-Quarter with Hal Martin as Cyril Overton, A. E. Raynor as Doctor Leslie Armstrong, Leigh Gabell as Godfrey Staunton, Cliff Davies as Lord Mount James.

The Mystery of Thor Bridge with A. B. Imeson as Neil Gibson, Noel Grahame as Dolores Gibson, Violet Graham as Miss Dunbar, Harry J. Worth as Inspector (Sergeant) Coventry.
The Mazarin Stone with Lionel d'Aragon as Count Sylvius, Tom Beaumont as Inspector Gregory, Laurie Leslie as Merton.
The Dancing Men with Frank Goldsmith as Hilton Cubitt, Dezma du May as Mrs Cubitt, Wally Bosco as Abe Slaney.
The Crooked Man with R. Lindsay as Major Murphy, Warwick Ward as Captain Barclay, Gladys Jennings as Mrs Barclay, Dora de Winton as Miss Morrison, Jack Hobbs as Henry Wood.
The Final Problem with Percy Standing as Moriarty, Tom Beaumont as Inspector Gregory.

THE SIGN OF FOUR
British film adaptation
adap & dir: Maurice Elvey
Eille Norwood as Sherlock Holmes
Arthur Cullin as Doctor Watson
Mme d'Esterre as Mrs Hudson
with Isobel Elsom as Mary Morstan, Fred Raynham as Abdullah Khan, Norman Page as Jonathan Small, Humbertson Wright as Thaddeus Sholto, Henry Wilson as Tonga, Arthur Bell as Inspector Athelney Jones (prod: The Stoll Picture Productions). Feature length.

THE RETURN OF SHERLOCK HOLMES
British stage production
by J. E. Harold-Terry and Arthur Rose, adap from *The Disappearance of Lady Frances Carfax*
Eille Norwood as Sherlock Holmes
H. G. Stoker as Doctor Watson
with Molly Kerr as Lady Frances Carfax, Arthur Cullin as the Reverend Doctor Schlessinger, Noel Dainton as the Hon. Philip Green, Lauderdale Maitland as Colonel Sebastian Moran. Opened Princes Theatre, Shaftesbury Avenue, London, on 9 October.

Clive Brook's Sherlock Holmes is in disguise as a musician on board ship in *The Return of Sherlock Holmes* (1929).

1929

DER HUND VON BASKERVILLE
German film adaptation
adap: Herbert Juttke, Georg C. Klaren from *The Hound of the Baskervilles*, dir: Richard Oswald
Carlyle Blackwell as Sherlock Holmes
Georges Seroff as Doctor Watson
with Fritz Rasp as Stapleton, Betty Bird as Beryl Stapleton, Alma Taylor as Mrs Barrymore, Alexander Murski, Livio Pavanelli, Valy Arnheim, Carla Bartheel, Jaro Fürth, Robert Garrison (prod: Erda Film).

THE RETURN OF SHERLOCK HOLMES
American film production
sc: Garrett Fort, Basil Dean, dir: Basil Dean
Clive Brook as Sherlock Holmes
H. Reeves-Smith as Doctor Watson
with Donald Crisp as Colonel Sebastian Moran, Betty Lawford, Charles Hay, Phillips Holmes, Harry T. Morey as Moriarty, Hubert Druce, Arthur Mack (prod: Paramount). Released August. Silent and talking versions (latter 71 minutes).

1930–1

THE ADVENTURES OF SHERLOCK HOLMES
American radio adaptations
William Gillette as Sherlock Holmes
(first in series)
Richard Gordon as Sherlock Holmes
(remainder of series)
Leigh Lovell as Doctor Watson
Thirty-five stories adapted by Edith Meiser: **Abbey Grange**, **Black Peter**, **The Blanched Soldier**, **The Boscombe Valley Mystery**, **Charles Augustus Milverton**, **The Copper Beeches**, **The Creeping Man**, **The Crooked Man**, **The Dancing Men**, **The Five Orange Pips**, **The Golden Pince-Nez**, **The Greek Interpreter**, **The Illustrious Client**, **The Lion's Mane**, **The Man with the Twisted Lip**, **The Mazarin Stone**, **The Missing Three-Quarter**, **The Musgrave Ritual**, **The Naval Treaty**, **The Noble Bachelor**, **The Norwood Builder**, **The Priory School**, **The Red-Headed League**, **The Reigate Squires**, **The Resident Patient**, **The Retired Colourman**, **A Scandal in Bohemia**, **The Six Napoleons**, **The Solitary Cyclist**, **The Speckled Band** (with Gillette), **The Stockbroker's Clerk**, **The Sussex Vampire**, **Thor Bridge**. Heard 20 October to 15 June.

1931

THE SLEEPING CARDINAL (USA: SHERLOCK HOLMES' FATAL HOUR)
British film production
sc: Cyril Twyford, H. Fowler Mear, based in part on *The Final Problem* and *The Empty House*, dir: Leslie Hiscott
Arthur Wontner as Sherlock Holmes
Ian Fleming as Doctor Watson
Minnie Rayner as Mrs Hudson
with Norman McKinnel as Colonel Henslow alias Moriarty, Leslie Perrins as Ronald Adair, Jane Welsh, Philip Hewland as Inspector Lestrade, Charles Paton, Louis Goodrich as Colonel Sebastian Moran (prod: Julius Hagen for Twickenham Film Studios, distributed by Warner Bros.). 84 minutes.

Eille Norwood and Hubert Willis as Holmes and Watson. Above, in *Silver Blaze* and right, a disguised Holmes coming to Watson's rescue in *The Disappearance of Lady Frances Carfax*.

THE SPECKLED BAND
British film adaptation
adap: W. P. Lipscomb, dir: Jack Raymond
Raymond Massey as Sherlock Holmes
Athole Stewart as Doctor Watson
Marie Ault as Mrs Hudson
with Lyn Harding as Doctor Grimesby Rylott, Angela Baddeley as Helen Stonor, Nancy Price, Stanley Lathbury, Charles Paton, Joyce Moore (prod: Herbert Wilcox for British & Dominion, distributed by W&F). 90 minutes.

1931–2

THE ADVENTURES OF SHERLOCK HOLMES
American radio adaptations/originals
Richard Gordon as Sherlock Holmes
Leigh Lovell as Doctor Watson
Second series of 32 stories adapted or devised by Edith Meiser, including from the canon: **The Beryl Coronet, The Bruce-Partington Plans, The Cardboard Box, A Case of Identity, The Devil's Foot, The Dying Detective, The Engineer's Thumb, The "Gloria Scott", The Hound of the Baskervilles** (in six episodes), **Lady Frances Carfax, The Red Circle, A Study in Scarlet** (in four episodes), **The Three Gables, The Three Garridebs, The Veiled Lodger, Wisteria Lodge, The Yellow Face**. Heard 17 September to 23 June.

1932

THE HOUND OF THE BASKERVILLES
British film adaptation
adap: V. Gareth Gundrey with additional dialogue by Edgar Wallace, dir: V. Gareth Gundrey
Robert Rendel as Sherlock Holmes
Frederick Lloyd as Doctor Watson
with John Stuart as Sir Henry Baskerville, Reginald Bach as Stapleton, Heather Angel as Beryl Stapleton, Wilfred Shine as Doctor Mortimer, Sam Livesey, Henry Hallatt as Barrymore, Sybil Jane as Mrs Barrymore, Elizabeth Vaughan, Leonard Hayes (prod: Michael Balcon for Gainsborough, distributed by Gaumont-British). 75 minutes.

THE MISSING REMBRANDT
British film production
sc: Cyril Twyford, H. Fowler Mear, dir: Leslie Hiscott
Arthur Wontner as Sherlock Holmes
Ian Fleming as Doctor Watson
Minnie Rayner as Mrs Hudson
with Francis L. Sullivan, Dini Galvani, Miles Mander, Jane Welsh, Anthony Holles, Herbert Lomas, Ben Welden, Takase, Philip Hewland as Inspector Lestrade (prod: Julius Hagen for Twickenham Film Studios, distributed by PDC). 84 minutes.

THE SIGN OF FOUR
British film adaptation
adap: W. P. Lipscomb, dir: Graham Cutts
Arthur Wontner as Sherlock Holmes
Ian Hunter as Doctor Watson
Clare Greet as Mrs Hudson
with Isla Bevan as Mary Morstan, Ben Soutten as Jonathan Small, Miles Malleson as Thaddeus Sholto, Herbert Lomas as Major Sholto, Gilbert Davis as Inspector Athelney Jones, Roy Emerton, Kynaston Reeves as Bartholomew Sholto, Edgar Norfolk, Togo as Tonga (prod: Rowland V. Lee for Associated Radio). 76 minutes.

Clive Brook as the detective in drag in *Sherlock Holmes* (1932), a disguise that fools Professor Moriarty.

SHERLOCK HOLMES
American film production
sc: Bertram Millhauser, dir: William K. Howard
Clive Brook as Sherlock Holmes
Reginald Owen as Doctor Watson
with Miriam Jordan as Alice Faulkner, Ernest Torrence as Moriarty, Herbert Mundin, Howard Leeds as Billy, Alan Mowbray, Herbert Mundin, Montague Shaw, Ivan Simpson, Lucien Prival, Roy D'Arcy, Stanley Fields, Eddie Dillon, Robert Graves, Brandon Hurst, Claude King (prod: Fox). 65 minutes.

1932–3

THE ADVENTURES OF SHERLOCK HOLMES
American radio adaptations/originals
Richard Gordon as Sherlock Holmes
Leigh Lovell as Doctor Watson
Third series of 31 stories adapted or devised by Edith Meiser, including from the canon: **The Blue Carbuncle, The Empty House, His Last Bow, The Second Stain, Shoscombe Old Place, The Sign of Four** (in six episodes), **The Three Students**. Heard 28 September to 31 May.

1933

THE HOLMESES OF BAKER STREET
British stage production
by Basil Mitchell, dir: Leon M. Lion
Felix Aylmer as Sherlock Holmes
Sir Nigel Playfair as Doctor Watson
with Rosemary Ames as Shirley Holmes, Eva Moore as Mrs Watson, Martin Walker, Vincent Holman, Alfred Clark, Henry Hallatt (prod: Bertie A. Meyer). Opened at Lyric Theatre, London, on 15 February. Adapted for Broadway by William Jourdan Rapp and Leonardo Bercovici and opened at the Masque Theater, New York, on 9 December 1936, directed by Reginald Bach with Cyril Scott as Holmes and Conway Wingfield as Watson.

A STUDY IN SCARLET
American film production
sc: Robert Florey with continuity and dialogue by Reginald Owen, dir: Edwin L. Marin
Reginald Owen as Sherlock Holmes
Warburton Gamble as Doctor Watson
Tempe Pigott as Mrs Hudson

with June Clyde, Anna May Wong, Alan Dinehart, John Warburton, J. M. Kerrigan, Alan Mowbray as Inspector Lestrade, Doris Lloyd, Cecil Reynolds, Halliwell Hobbes, Tetsu Komai, Wyndham Standing (prod: E. W. Hammons for World Wide). 75 minutes.

1934–5

THE ADVENTURES OF SHERLOCK HOLMES
American radio series
Louis Hector as Sherlock Holmes
Leigh Lovell as Doctor Watson
Fourth series of 29 broadcasts written by Edith Meiser, probably all originals. Heard 11 November to 26 May.

1935

THE TRIUMPH OF SHERLOCK HOLMES
British film adaptation
adap: H. Fowler Mear, Cyril Twyford, from *The Valley of Fear*, dir: Leslie S. Hiscott
Arthur Wontner as Sherlock Holmes
Ian Fleming as Doctor Watson
Minnie Rayner as Mrs Hudson
with Lyn Harding as Moriarty, Leslie Perrins as John Douglas, Jane Carr as Ettie Douglas, Charles Mortimer as Inspector Lestrade, Michael Shepley as Cecil Barker, Ben Welden, Roy Emerton, Conway Dixon, Wilfred Caithness as Colonel Sebastian Moran, Edmund D'Alby, Ernest Lynds (prod: Julius Hagen for Real Art, distributed by Gaumont-British). 84 minutes.

SHERLOCK HOLMES
American radio adaptation
adap: Edith Meiser from the play by William Gillette and Arthur Conan Doyle
William Gillette as Sherlock Holmes
Reginald Mason as Doctor Watson
with Charles Bryant as Moriarty, Betty Hanna as Alice Faulkner, Reynolds Denniston, William Postance. Heard 18 November.

1936

SHERLOCK HOLMES
American radio adaptations/originals
Richard Gordon as Sherlock Holmes
Harry West as Doctor Watson
Series of 48 stories adapted or devised by Edith Meiser, including the following from the canon: **The Beryl Coronet, Black Peter, The Blanched Soldier, The Blue Carbuncle, The Cardboard Box, The Creeping Man, The Dancing Men, The Devil's Foot, The Dying Detective, The Empty House, The Golden Pince-Nez, The Illustrious Client, The Lion's Mane, The Man with the Twisted Lip, The Mazarin Stone, The Missing Three-Quarter, The Musgrave Ritual, The Naval Treaty, The Noble Bachelor, The Norwood Builder, The Red-Headed League, The Reigate Squires, The Resident Patient, The Retired Colourman, A Scandal in Bohemia, The Second Stain, Silver Blaze, The Six Napoleons, The Solitary Cyclist, The Speckled Band, The Stockbroker's Clerk, The Sussex Vampire, Thor Bridge, Wisteria Lodge**. Heard 1 October to 24 December.

1937

DER HUND VON BASKERVILLE
German film adaptation
adap: Carla von Stackelberg from *The Hound of the Baskervilles*, dir: Carl Lamac
Bruno Güttner as Sherlock Holmes
Fritz Odemar as Doctor Watson
Gertrud Wolle as Mrs Hudson
with Peter Voss as Lord Henry Baskerville, Erich Ponto as Stapleton, Ernst Rotmund as Doctor Mortimer, Alice Brandt as Beryl Stapleton, Lilly Schönborn as Mrs Barrymore, Fritz Rasp as Barrymore, Hanna Waag, Friedrich Kayssler, Artur Malkowski, Paul Rehkopf as Selden, Klaus Pohl, Horst Birr, Ernst A. Schaah, Ika Thimm, Kurt Lauermann (prod: Ondra-Lamac Film).

SILVER BLAZE
(USA: **MURDER AT THE BASKERVILLES**)
British film adaptation
adap: Arthur Macrae, H. Fowler Mear, dir: Thomas Bentley
Arthur Wontner as Sherlock Holmes
Ian Fleming as Doctor Watson
Minnie Rayner as Mrs Hudson
with Lyn Harding as Moriarty, John Turnbull as Inspector Lestrade, Robert Horton as Colonel Ross, Lawrence Grossmith as Sir Henry Baskerville, Judy Gunn, Arthur Macrae, Arthur Goullet as Colonel Sebastian Moran, Martin Walker as John Straker, Eve Gray as Mrs Straker, Gilbert Davies, D. J. Williams as Silas Brown, Ralph Truman, Ronald Shiner (prod: Julius Hagen for Twickenham Film Productions, distributed by Associated British). 70 minutes.

1938

SHERLOCK HOLMES
American radio adaptation
in series *The Mercury Theatre on the Air*, adap from the play by William Gillette and Arthur Conan Doyle & dir: Orson Welles
Orson Welles as Sherlock Holmes
Ray Collins as Doctor Watson
with Eustace Wyatt as Moriarty, Mary Taylor as Alice Faulkner, Edgar Barrier, Richard Wilson, Brenda Forbes, Morgan Fowley, Alfred Shirley, William Allen, Arthur Anderson. Heard 25 September.

1939–46

American film series
Basil Rathbone as Sherlock Holmes
Nigel Bruce as Doctor Watson
Mary Gordon as Mrs Hudson

Two films from 20th Century-Fox, produced by Gene Markey

THE HOUND OF THE BASKERVILLES (1939)
adap: Ernest Pascal, dir: Sidney Lanfield
with Richard Greene as Sir Henry Baskerville, Wendy Barrie as Beryl Stapleton, Lionel Atwill as Doctor Mortimer, Morton Lowry as Stapleton, John Carradine as Barryman (Barrymore), Nigel De Brulier as Selden, Eily Malyon as Mrs Barryman (Barrymore). Released March. 80 minutes.

THE ADVENTURES OF SHERLOCK HOLMES (1939)
sc: Edwin Blum, William Drake, dir: Alfred Werker
with Ida Lupino, Alan Marshall, Terry Kilburn as Billy, George Zucco as Professor Moriarty, Henry Stephenson, E. E. Clive, George Regas, Arthur Hohl. Released August. 82 minutes.

Twelve films from Universal
Dennis Hoey as Inspector Lestrade

SHERLOCK HOLMES AND THE VOICE OF TERROR (1942)
sc: Lynn Riggs, John Bright, Robert D. Andrews, dir: John Rawlins
with Evelyn Ankers, Reginald Denny, Henry Daniell, Montagu Love, Thomas Gomez, Hillary Brooke. Released September. 65 minutes.

SHERLOCK HOLMES AND THE SECRET WEAPON (1942)
sc: Edward T. Lowe, W. Scott Darling, Edmund L. Hartmann, dir: Roy William Neill
with Kaaren Verne, Lionel Atwill as Professor Moriarty, William Post Jr., Holmes Herbert. Released December. 68 minutes.

SHERLOCK HOLMES IN WASHINGTON (1943)
sc: Bertram Millhauser, Lynn Riggs, dir: Roy William Neill
with Marjorie Lord, Henry Daniell, George Zucco, John Archer, Gavin Muir, Edmund Mac-Donald, Holmes Herbert, Thurston Hall, Gilbert Emery. Released March. 71 minutes.

SHERLOCK HOLMES FACES DEATH (1943)
sc: Bertram Millhauser, from *The Musgrave Ritual*, dir: Roy William Neill
with Hillary Brooke, Milburn Stone, Arthur Margetson, Halliwell Hobbes as Brunton, Gavin Muir, Frederick Worlock, Olaf Hytten, Gerald Hamer, Vernon Downing, Norma Varden. Released September. 68 minutes.

THE SCARLET CLAW (1944)
sc: Edmund L. Hartmann, Roy William Neill, from story by Paul Gangelin, Brenda Weisberg, dir: Roy William Neill
with Gerald Hamer, Paul Cavanagh, Arthur Hohl, Miles Mander, Kay Harding, David Clyde, Ian Wolfe, Victoria Horne. Released April. 74 minutes.

SHERLOCK HOLMES AND THE SPIDER WOMAN (1944)
(Britain: **SPIDER WOMAN**)
sc: Bertram Millhauser, dir: Roy William Neill
with Gale Sondergaard, Vernon Downing, Alec Craig, Arthur Hohl. Released January. 62 minutes.

THE PEARL OF DEATH (1944)
sc: Bertram Millhauser, from *The Six Napoleons*, dir: Roy William Neill
with Evelyn Ankers, Miles Mander, Ian Wolfe, Charles Francis, Rondo Hatton, Holmes Herbert. Released September. 69 minutes.

THE HOUSE OF FEAR (1945)
sc: Roy Chanslor, dir: Roy William Neill
with Aubrey Mather, Paul Cavanagh, Holmes Herbert, Harry Cording, Sally Shepherd, Gavin Muir, Florette Hillier, David Clyde, Wilson Benge, Alec Craig. Released March. 67 minutes.

THE WOMAN IN GREEN (1945)
sc: Bertram Millhauser, dir: Roy Willam Neill
with Hillary Brooke, Henry Daniell as Professor Moriarty, Paul Cavanagh, Matthew Boulton as Inspector Gregson, Frederick Worlock, Sally Shepherd, Olaf Hytten. Released July. 68 minutes.

PURSUIT TO ALGIERS (1945)
sc: Leonard Lee, dir: Roy William Neill
with Marjorie Riordan, Rosalind Ivan, Martin Kosleck, John Abbott, Frederick Worlock, Morton Lowry, Leslie Vincent, Gerald Hamer, Rex Evans. Released October. 65 minutes.

TERROR BY NIGHT (1946)
sc: Frank Gruber, dir: Roy William Neill
with Alan Mowbray as Colonel Sebastian Moran alias Major Duncan Bleek, Renee Godfrey, Mary Forbes, Billy Bevan, Frederick Worlock, Geoffrey Steele, Boyd Davis, Skelton Knaggs, Gerald Hamer, Harry Cording. Released February. 60 minutes.

DRESSED TO KILL (1946)
(Britain: **SHERLOCK HOLMES AND THE SECRET CODE**)
sc: Leonard Lee, Frank Gruber, dir: Roy William Neill
with Patricia Morison, Edmond Breon, Frederick Worlock, Carl Harbord as Inspector Hopkins, Harry Cording, Ian Wolfe. Released June. 72 minutes.

Rathbone and Bruce additionally appeared as Holmes and Watson in a guest appearance in Universal's 1943 Olsen and Johnson comedy *Crazy House*.

1939–40

THE ADVENTURES OF SHERLOCK HOLMES
American radio adaptations
Basil Rathbone as Sherlock Holmes
Nigel Bruce as Doctor Watson
Series of 24 stories adapted by Edith Meiser: **Abbey Grange, The Beryl Coronet, The Blanched Soldier, The Blue Carbuncle, The Bruce-Partington Plans, The Cardboard Box, Charles Augustus Milverton, The Creeping Man, The Devil's Foot, The Dying Detective, The Greek Interpreter, The Lion's Mane, The Man with the Twisted Lip, The Musgrave Ritual, The Priory School, The Reigate Squires,**

The Retired Colourman, The Second Stain, Shoscombe Old Place, Silver Blaze, The Speckled Band, The Sussex Vampire, The Three Garridebs, Wisteria Lodge. Heard 2 October to 11 March.

1940–1

SHERLOCK HOLMES
American radio adaptations
Basil Rathbone as Sherlock Holmes
Nigel Bruce as Doctor Watson
Series of 19 stories, all but one adapted by Edith Meiser from the canon: **Black Peter, The Boscombe Valley Mystery, The Copper Beeches, The Crooked Man, The Dancing Men, The Empty House, The Engineer's Thumb, The Hound of the Baskervilles** (in six episodes), **The Mazarin Stone, The Missing Three-Quarter, The Naval Treaty, The Noble Bachelor, The Red-Headed League, The Resident Patient, Shoscombe Old Place, The Speckled Band, Thor Bridge, The Three Students.**

1941–2

SHERLOCK HOLMES
American radio adaptations/originals
Basil Rathbone as Sherlock Holmes
Nigel Bruce as Doctor Watson
Series of 22 stories adapted or devised by Edith Meiser, including the following from the canon: **A Case of Identity, The Devil's Foot, The Five Orange Pips, The "Gloria Scott", The Illustrious Client, The Lion's Mane, The Second Stain, The Six Napoleons, The Solitary Cyclist, The Stockbroker's Clerk, The Sussex Vampire, The Three Gables.** Heard 5 October to 1 March.

1943

SHERLOCK HOLMES
American radio adaptations/originals
Basil Rathbone as Sherlock Holmes
Nigel Bruce as Doctor Watson
Series of 23 stories adapted or devised by Edith Meiser, including the following from the canon: **The Bruce-Partington Plans, The Cardboard Box, The Copper Beeches, The Creeping Man, The Devil's Foot, The Dying Detective, The Engineer's Thumb, The Greek Interpreter, The Man with the Twisted Lip, The Musgrave Ritual, The Priory School, The Red-Headed League, The Retired Colourman, Silver Blaze, The Speckled Band, Wisteria Lodge.** Heard 30 April to 1 October.

THE BOSCOMBE VALLEY MYSTERY
British radio adaptation
adap: Ashley Sampson
Arthur Wontner as Sherlock Holmes
Carleton Hobbs as Doctor Watson
with Ronald Kerr as Charles McCarthy, Alan Blair as James McCarthy, Deryck Guyler as John Turner, Moira Lister as Miss Turner, Arthur Bush as Inspector Lestrade (prod: Howard Rose for BBC Home Service). Heard 3 July. 50 minutes.

1943–5

SHERLOCK HOLMES
American radio adaptations/originals
Basil Rathbone as Sherlock Holmes
Nigel Bruce as Doctor Watson
Series of 87 stories adapted or devised by Bruce Taylor (Leslie Charteris), Denis Green and

Anthony Boucher, including the following from the canon: **The Blue Carbuncle, The Bruce-Partington Plans, The Devil's Foot, Lady Frances Carfax, The Man with the Twisted Lip.** Heard 4 October 1943 to 28 May 1945.

1945

THE ADVENTURE OF THE SPECKLED BAND
British radio adaptation
adap: John Dickson Carr
Cedric Hardwicke as Sherlock Holmes
Finlay Currie as Doctor Watson
Dora Gregory as Mrs Hudson
with Richard George as Doctor Grimesby Roylott, Grizelda Hervey as Helen Stoner, Thea Wells as Julia Stoner (prod: Martyn C. Webster for BBC Home Service). Heard 17 May. 30 minutes.

1945–6

SHERLOCK HOLMES
American radio adaptations/originals
Basil Rathbone as Sherlock Holmes
Nigel Bruce as Doctor Watson
Series of 38 stories adapted or devised by Denis Green and Anthony Boucher, including the following from the canon: **The Man with the Twisted Lip, A Scandal in Bohemia, The Speckled Band, Thor Bridge.** Heard 3 September to 27 May.

1946–7

THE NEW ADVENTURES OF SHERLOCK HOLMES
American radio adaptations/originals
Tom Conway as Sherlock Holmes
Nigel Bruce as Doctor Watson
Series of 39 stories adapted or devised by Denis Green and Anthony Boucher, including the following from the canon: **The Dying Detective, The Red-Headed League, The Speckled Band.** Heard 12 October to 7 July.

1947–8

SHERLOCK HOLMES
American radio adaptations/originals
John Stanley as Sherlock Holmes
Alfred Shirley as Doctor Watson
Series of 39 stories adapted or devised by Edith Meiser, including the following from the canon: **A Case of Identity, The Copper Beeches, The Engineer's Thumb, Lady Frances Carfax, The Mazarin Stone, The Naval Treaty, The Red-Headed League, Shoscombe Old Place, The Six Napoleons, The Sussex Vampire, The Veiled Lodger.** Heard 28 September to 20 June.

1948–9

SHERLOCK HOLMES
American radio adaptations/originals
John Stanley as Sherlock Holmes
Ian Martin as Doctor Watson
Series of 37 stories adapted or devised by Howard Merrill and others, including the following from the canon: **Black Peter, The Blue Carbuncle, The Devil's Foot, The Golden Pince-Nez.** Heard 12 September to 6 June.

1949–50

THE ADVENTURES OF SHERLOCK HOLMES
American radio adaptations/originals
Ben Wright as Sherlock Holmes
Eric Snowden as Doctor Watson
Series of stories adapted or devised by Denis Green. Heard 21 September to 14 June.

1951

THE MAN WITH THE TWISTED LIP
British film/television adaptation
dir: Richard M. Grey
John Longden as Sherlock Holmes
Campbell Singer as Doctor Watson
with Hector Ross as Neville St Clair, Beryl Baxter, Walter Gotell (prod: Rudolph Cartier for Vandyke/Telecine, distributed by Grand National). Released March. 35 minutes.

British television adaptations
Alan Wheatley as Sherlock Holmes
Raymond Francis as Doctor Watson
Bill Owen as Inspector Lestrade
Iris Vandeleur as Mrs Hudson
Six stories adapted for live television by C. A. Lejeune and produced by Ian Atkins, each 35 minutes long.
The Empty House with Eric Maturin as Colonel Moran. Shown 20 October.
A Scandal in Bohemia with Alan Judd as the King of Bohemia, Olga Edwards as Irene Adler, John Stevens as Godfrey Norton. Shown 27 October.
The Dying Detective with Henry Oscar as Culverton Smith. Shown 3 November.

The Reigate Squires with Thomas Heathcote as Alec Cunningham, Becket Bould as Mr Cunningham, H. G. Stoker as Colonel Hayter, Stanley Van Beers as Inspector Forrester. Shown 17 November.
The Red-Headed League with Sebastian Cabot as Jabez Wilson, Martin Starkie as Vincent Spaulding, Larry Burne as Duncan Ross, Arthur Goulett as Mr Merryweather. Shown 24 November.
The Second Stain with John Robinson as Trelawney Hope, Alvys Maben as Lady Hilda, J. Leslie Firth as the Premier, John Le Mesurier as Eduardo Lucas, Donald Kemp as P. C. Macpherson. Shown 1 December.

1953

SHERLOCK HOLMES
British radio adaptation
adap: Raymond Raikes from the play by William Gillette and Arthur Conan Doyle
Carleton Hobbs as Sherlock Holmes
Norman Shelley as Doctor Watson
with Frederick Valk as Moriarty, Sarah Leigh as Alice Faulkner, Jonathan Field as Billy, Allan Jeayes, Valentine Dyall, Catherine Salkeld (prod: Raymond Raikes for BBC Home Service). Heard 3 January, repeated 8 January.

THE GREAT DETECTIVE
British ballet production
choreography by Margaret Dale, music by Richard Arnell

Kenneth Macmillan as "The Great Detective" and "The Infamous Professor"
Stanley Holden as "His Friend the Doctor"
with David Blair. Opened 21 January, Sadler's Wells Theatre, London.

THE ADVENTURE OF THE BLACK BARONET
American television production
in series, *Suspense*, adap: Michael Dyne from the story by Adrian Conan Doyle and John Dickson Carr, dir: Robert Mulligan
Basil Rathbone as Sherlock Holmes
Martyn Green as Doctor Watson
with Mary Howard, Anthony Dearden (prod: Martin Manulis). Shown (live) 26 May. 23 minutes.

SHERLOCK HOLMES
American stage production
by Ouida Rathbone, dir: Reginald Denham
Basil Rathbone as Sherlock Holmes
Jack Raine as Doctor Watson
Elwyn Harvey as Mrs Hudson
with Jarmila Novotna as Irene Adler, Thomas Gomez as Moriarty, John Dodsworth as the Rt Hon Trelawney Hope, Eileen Peel as Lady Hope, Chester Stratton, Terence Kilburn, Mary Orr as

The original British poster and the French version for the 1959 *Hound of the Baskervilles*.

Miss Dunbar, Gregory Morton as Eduardo Lucas, Richard Wendley as Arthur Cadogan West, Margit Forssgren, Bryan Herbert as Inspector Lestrade, Evan Thomas, Martin Brandt as Count Hugo Oberstein, Ludwig Roth, St John Phillipe, Arthur N. Stenning, Alfred A. Hesse (prod: Bill Doll). Opened 30 October, Century Theater, New York.

1954

THE ADVENTURES OF SHERLOCK HOLMES
British radio adaptations
John Gielgud as Sherlock Holmes
Ralph Richardson as Doctor Watson
Series of 12 stories adapted by John Keir Cross, directed by either Val Gielgud or Martyn C. Webster, and produced by Harry Alan Towers: **The Blue Carbuncle**, **The Bruce-Partington Plans** (with Val Gielgud as Mycroft Holmes), **A Case of Identity**, **Charles Augustus Milverton** (in *Doctor Watson Meets Sherlock Holmes* with John Cazabon as Inspector Lestrade), **The Dying Detective** (with Elizabeth Maude as Mrs Hudson), **The Final Problem** (with Orson Welles as Moriarty), **The Norwood Builder**, **The Red-Headed League**, **A Scandal in Bohemia** (with Margaret Ward as Irene Adler), **The Second Stain**, **The Six Napoleons**, **The Solitary Cyclist**. Heard 5 October to 21 December (America: from 20 February 1955). Each 30 minutes.

American television series (made in France)
Ronald Howard as Sherlock Holmes
Howard Marion Crawford as Doctor Watson
Archie Duncan as Inspector Lestrade
Series of 39 stories made by Guild Films (prod: Nicole Milinaire), mostly directed by Sheldon Reynolds, each 27 minutes long, all seemingly original scripts except:
The Red-Headed League adap: Lou Morheim, dir: Sheldon Reynolds with Alexander Gauge as Jabez Wilson, Eugene Deckers as Vincent Spaulding, Colin Drake as Duncan Ross, M. Seyford as Mr Merryweather.

1958

THE HOUND OF THE BASKERVILLES
British radio adaptation
adap: Felix Felton
Carleton Hobbs as Sherlock Holmes
Norman Shelley as Doctor Watson
with Paul Eddington as Doctor Mortimer, Ronald Wilson as Sir Henry Baskerville, Lewis Gedge as Barrymore, Rolf Lefebvre as Stapleton, Pamela Alan as Beryl Stapleton, Paul Lorraine as Inspector Lestrade (prod: Patrick Dromgoole). Heard in six 30-minute episodes, 6 April to 11 May.

1959

THE HOUND OF THE BASKERVILLES
British film adaptation
adap: Peter Bryan, dir: Terence Fisher
Peter Cushing as Sherlock Holmes
Andre Morell as Doctor Watson
with Christopher Lee as Sir Henry Baskerville, Marla Landi as Cecile (Beryl) Stapleton, Francis de Wolff as Doctor Mortimer, Ewen Solon as Stapleton, John Le Mesurier as Barrymore, Michael Mulcaster as Selden, Helen Goss as Mrs Barrymore (prod: Anthony Hinds for Hammer Films, distributed by United Artists). Released March. 87 minutes.

SHERLOCK HOLMES
British radio adaptations
Carleton Hobbs as Sherlock Holmes
Norman Shelley as Doctor Watson
Series of six stories adapted by Michael Hardwick: **The Beryl Coronet**, **The Blanched Soldier**, **The Copper Beeches**, **The Man with the Twisted Lip**, **The Noble Bachelor**, **Shoscombe Old Place**. Heard 12 May to 25 August.

THE SIGN OF FOUR
British radio adaptation
adap: Felix Felton
Richard Hurndall as Sherlock Holmes
Bryan Coleman as Doctor Watson
Elsa Palmer as Mrs Hudson
with Barbara Mitchell as Mary Morstan, Haydn Jones as Inspector Athelney Jones, Paul Taylor as Wiggins, Leigh Crutchley as Jonathan Small, John Moffatt as Thaddeus Sholto (prod: Archie Campbell for BBC Light Programme). Heard in five 30-minute episodes 16 May to 13 June.

1960

SHERLOCK HOLMES
British radio adaptations
Carleton Hobbs as Sherlock Holmes
Norman Shelley as Doctor Watson
Humphrey Morton as Inspector Lestrade
Series of seven stories adapted by Michael Hardwick and produced by Michael Hardwick: **The Cardboard Box**, **The Engineer's Thumb**, **The Greek Interpreter**, **The Illustrious Client**, **Lady Frances Carfax**, **The Naval Treaty**, **The Stockbroker's Clerk**. Heard 23 February to 31 May.

THE VALLEY OF FEAR
adap: Michael Hardwick
with Penelope Lee as Mrs Hudson, Duncan McIntyre as Inspector MacDonald, Valerie Hanson as Ivy Douglas, Lee Fox as John Douglas, George Hagan as Cecil Barker (prod: Robin Midgley). Heard 31 December. 90 minutes.

1961–2

SHERLOCK HOLMES
British radio adaptations
Carleton Hobbs as Sherlock Holmes
Norman Shelley as Doctor Watson
Series of six stories adapted by Michael Hardwick: **Charles Augustus Milverton**, **The Empty House**, **The Priory School**, **The Reigate Squires**, **The Resident Patient**, **Thor Bridge**. Heard 27 November to 8 January.

Series of eight stories adapted by Michael Hardwick: **Abbey Grange**, **The Devil's Foot**, **The Golden Pince-Nez**, **The Mazarin Stone**, **The Missing Three-Quarter**, **The Musgrave Ritual**, **Silver Blaze**, **The Speckled Band**. Heard 17 July to 4 September.

A STUDY IN SCARLET
adap: Michael Hardwick
with Barbara Mitchell as Mrs Hudson, Humphrey Morton as Inspector Gregson, Godfrey Kenton as Inspector Lestrade, Stuart Nichol as Jefferson Hope (prod: Norman Wright). Heard 22 December. 90 minutes.

1962

SHERLOCK HOLMES UND DAS HALSBAND DES TODES
(English title: **SHERLOCK HOLMES AND THE DEADLY NECKLACE**)
German film production
sc: Curt Siodmak, dir: Terence Fisher
Christopher Lee as Sherlock Holmes
Thorley Walters as Doctor Watson
Edith Schultze-Westrum as Mrs Hudson
with Hans Söhnker as Moriarty, Hans Nielsen, Senta Berger, Ivan Desny, Leon Askin, Wolfgang Lukschy, Bernard Lajarrige (prod: Artur Brauner for CCC/Criterion/INCEI. 86 minutes.

1963

THE SIGN OF FOUR
British radio adaptation
adap: Michael Hardwick
Carleton Hobbs as Sherlock Holmes
Norman Shelley as Doctor Watson
Grizelda Hervey as Mrs Hudson
with Elizabeth Morgan as Mary Morstan, Philip Leaver as Thaddeus Sholto, George Merritt as Inspector Athelney Jones, Malcolm Hayes as Jonathan Small (prod: Val Gielgud). Heard 2 March. 90 minutes.

1964

THE SPECKLED BAND
British television adaptation
in series *Detective*, adap: Giles Cooper, dir: Robin Midgley
Douglas Wilmer as Sherlock Holmes
Nigel Stock as Doctor Watson
Mary Holder as Mrs Hudson
with Felix Felton as Doctor Grimesby Roylott, Liane Aukin as Helen Stoner, Donald Douglas as Percy Armitage. Shown 18 May. 50 minutes.

SHERLOCK HOLMES RETURNS
British radio adaptations
Carleton Hobbs as Sherlock Holmes
Norman Shelley as Doctor Watson
Humphrey Morton as Inspector Lestrade
Series of 10 stories adapted by Michael Hardwick: **Abbey Grange**, **The Bruce-Partington Plans**, **The Mazarin Stone**, **The Norwood Builder**, **The Red-Headed League**, **The Retired Colourman**, **The Solitary Cyclist**, **The Sussex Vampire**, **The Three Gables**, **The Three Garridebs**. Heard 7 August to 9 October.

1965

BAKER STREET
American musical production
book by Jerome Coopersmith, music and lyrics by Marian Grudeff and Raymond Jessel, dir: Harold Prince
Fritz Weaver as Sherlock Holmes
Peter Sallis as Doctor Watson
Paddy Edwards as Mrs Hudson
with Inga Swenson as Irene Adler, Martin Gabel as Moriarty, Patrick Horgan, Martin Wolfson, Joe Bennett as Wiggins, Daniel Keyes as Inspector Lestrade, Virginia Vestoff, Bert Michaels, Sal Pernice, George Lee, Mark Jude Sheil, George Fisher, Avin Harum, Tommy Tune, Ross-Miles, Gwenn Lewis (prod: Alexander H. Cohen). Opened 14 February, Broadway Theater, New York.

British television adaptations
Douglas Wilmer as Sherlock Holmes
Nigel Stock as Doctor Watson
Peter Madden as Inspector Lestrade
Enid Lindsey as Mrs Hudson
Twelve stories produced by David Goddard for BBC TV, each 50 minutes.

The Illustrious Client (adap: Giles Cooper, dir: Peter Sasdy) with Peter Wyngarde as Baron Gruner, Rosemary Leach as Kitty Winter, Jennie Linden as Violet de Merville. Shown 20 February.

The Devil's Foot (adap: Giles Cooper, dir: Max Varnel) with Patrick Troughton as Mortimer Tregennis. Shown 27 February.

The Copper Beeches (adap: Vincent Tilsley, dir: Gareth Davies) with Patrick Wymark as Jephro Rucastle, Suzanne Neve as Violet Hunter. Shown 6 March.

The Red-Headed League (adap: Anthony Read, dir: Peter Duguid) with Toke Townley as Jabez Wilson, David Andrews as Vincent Spaulding, John Barcroft as Inspector Hopkins. Shown 13 March.

The Abbey Grange (adap: Clifford Witting, dir: Peter Cregeen) with Nyree Dawn Porter as Lady Brackenstall, Peter Jesson as Captain Croker, John Barcroft as Inspector Hopkins. Shown 20 March.

The Six Napoleons (adap: Giles Cooper, dir: Gareth Davies) with Arthur Hewlett as Josiah Brown. Shown 27 March.

The Man with the Twisted Lip (adap: Jan Read, dir: Eric Taylor) with Anton Rodgers as Hugh Boone/Neville St Clair, Anna Cropper as Mrs St Clair. Shown 3 April.

The Beryl Coronet (adap: Nicholas Palmer, dir: Max Varnel) with Leonard Sachs as Alexander Holder, Richard Carpenter as Arthur, Suzan Farmer as Mary, David Burke as Sir George Burnwell. Shown 10 April.

The Bruce-Partington Plans (adap: Giles Cooper, dir: Shaun Sutton) with Derek Francis as Mycroft Holmes, Allan Cuthbertson as Colonel Valentine Walter, Carl Duering as Herr Oberstein. Shown 17 April.

Charles Augustus Milverton (adap: Clifford Witting, dir: Philip Dudley) with Barry Jones as Milverton, Penelope Horner as Lady Eva Brackwell, Ann Penfold as Agatha. Shown 24 April.

The Retired Colourman (adap: Jan Read, dir: Michael Hayes) with Maurice Denham as Josiah Amberley. Shown 1 May.

The Disappearance of Lady Frances Carfax (adap: Vincent Tilsley, dir: Shaun Sutton) with Joss Ackland as the Hon. Philip Green, Ronald Radd as Doctor Shlessinger, Sheila Shand Gibbs as Lady Frances Carfax. Shown 8 May.

A STUDY IN TERROR
British film production
sc: Donald and Derek Ford, dir: James Hill
John Neville as Sherlock Holmes
Donald Houston as Doctor Watson
Barbara Leake as Mrs Hudson
with John Fraser, Anthony Quayle, Barbara Windsor, Adrienne Corri, Frank Finlay as Inspector Lestrade, Judi Dench, Peter Carsten, Charles Regnier, Robert Morley as Mycroft Holmes, Cecil Parker, Georgia Brown, Barry Jones, Terry Downes, John Cairney, Kay Walsh, Edina Ronay, Avis Bunnage, Patrick Newell, Liz Stride (prod: Herman Cohen, Henry E. Lester for Compton/Tekli/Sir Nigel). Opened November. 95 minutes.

Holmes and Lestrade: John Neville and Frank Finlay in *A Study in Terror* (1965).

1966–7

SHERLOCK HOLMES AGAIN
British radio adaptations
Carleton Hobbs as Sherlock Holmes
Norman Shelley as Doctor Watson
Series of nine stories adapted by Michael Hardwick and produced by Martyn C. Webster: **The Boscombe Valley Mystery**, **The Crooked Man**, **The Dying Detective**, **The Final Problem** (with Rolf Lefevbre as Moriarty), **The Five Orange Pips**, **A Scandal in Bohemia** (with Gudrun Ure as Irene Adler), **The Second Stain**, **The Six Napoleons**, **Wisteria Lodge**. Heard 21 November to 16 January.

1968

British television adaptations
Peter Cushing as Sherlock Holmes
Nigel Stock as Doctor Watson
Grace Arnold as Mrs Hudson
Fifteen stories produced by William Sterling, each 50 minutes (except *Hound of the Baskervilles*, 100 minutes).

The Second Stain (adap: Jennifer Stuart, dir: Henri Safran) with Daniel Massey as Trelawney Hope, Cecil Parker as Lord Bellinger, Penelope Horner as Lady Hilda, William Lucas as Inspector Lestrade. Shown 9 September.

The Dancing Men. Shown 16 September.

A Study in Scarlet (adap: Hugh Leonard, dir: Henri Safran) with George A. Cooper as Inspector

Gregson, William Lucas as Inspector Lestrade, Tony McLaren as Wiggins, Larry Cross as Jefferson Hope.

The Hound of the Baskervilles (adap: Hugh Leonard, dir: Graham Evans) with Gary Raymond as Sir Henry Baskerville, Gabriella Licudi as Beryl Stapleton, Philip Bond as Stapleton, David Leland as Doctor Mortimer, Christopher Burgess as Barrymore. Shown 30 September and 7 October in two parts.

The Boscombe Valley Mystery (adap: Bruce Stewart, dir: Viktors Ritelis) with John Tate as Turner, Nick Tate as James McCarthy. Shown 14 October.

The Greek Interpreter (adap: John Gould, dir: David Saire) with Peter Woodthorpe as Wilson Kemp, Nigel Terry as Harold Latimer, Ronald Adam as Mycroft Holmes, George A. Cooper as Inspector Gregson, Clive Cazes as Melas. Shown 21 October.

The Naval Treaty (adap: John Gould, dir: Antony Kearey) with Dennis Price as Lord Holdhurst, Corin Redgrave as Percy Phelps, Peter Bowles as Joseph Harrison, Jane Lapotaire as Annie Harrison. Shown 28 October.

Thor Bridge (adap: Harry Moore, dir: Antony Kearey) with Juliet Mills as Grace Dunbar, Isa Miranda as Dolores, Grant Taylor as Neil Gibson. Shown 4 November.

The Musgrave Ritual (adap: Alexander Baron, dir: Viktors Ritelis) with Georgia Brown as Rachel, Norman Wooland as Reginald Musgrave, Brian Jackson as Brunton. Shown 11 November.

Black Peter (adap: Richard Harris, dir: Antony Kearey) with Ilona Rogers as Rachel Carey, James Kenney as Inspector Hopkins, John Tate as Peter Carey. Shown 18 November.

Wisteria Lodge (adap: Alexander Baron, dir: Roger Jenkins) with Richard Pearson as Inspector Baynes, Derek Francis as John Scott Eccles, Carlos Pierre as Garcia, Walter Gotell as Henderson, Christopher Carlos as Lucas. Shown 25 November.

Shoscombe Old Place (dir: Bill Bain) with Nigel Green as Sir Robert Norberton, Edward Woodward as Mason. Shown 2 December.

The Solitary Cyclist (adap: Stanley Miller, dir: Viktors Ritelis) with Carole Potter as Violet Smith, Charles Tingwell as Carruthers, David Butler as Woodley. Shown 9 December.

The Sign of Four (adap: Michael and Mollie Hardwick, dir: William Sterling) with Ann Bell as Mary Morstan, Paul Daneman as Thaddeus and Bartholomew Sholto, John Stratton as Inspector Athelney Jones, Howard Goornay as Jonathan Small, Tony McLaren as Wiggins, Zen Keller as Tonga. Shown 16 December.

The Blue Carbuncle (adap: Stanley Miller, dir: Bill Bain) with Madge Ryan as Lady Morcar, James Beck as James Ryder, Neil Fitzpatrick as John Horner, Ernest Hare as Windigate, Frank Middlemass as Peterson, Michael Robbins as Breckinridge. Shown 23 December.

Peter Cushing's Holmes discusses with Nigel Stock's Watson the warning message sent to Sir Henry Baskerville at his London hotel in *The Hound of the Baskervilles* (1968).

1969

SHERLOCK HOLMES

British radio adaptations

Carleton Hobbs as Sherlock Holmes
Norman Shelley as Doctor Watson
Series of six stories adapted by Michael Hardwick:
Black Peter, **A Case of Identity**, **The Dancing Men**, **His Last Bow**, **The Lion's Mane**, **The Red Circle**. Heard 24 June to 10 July.

1970

THE PRIVATE LIFE OF SHERLOCK HOLMES

American film production (shot in England)
sc: Billy Wilder and I. A. L. Diamond, dir: Billy Wilder
Robert Stephens as Sherlock Holmes
Colin Blakely as Doctor Watson
Irene Handl as Mrs Hudson
with Christopher Lee as Mycroft Holmes, Genevieve Page, Clive Revill, Tamara Toumanova, Catherine Lacey, Mollie Maureen, Peter Madden (prod: Billy Wilder for Phalanx/Mirisch/Sir Nigel, distributed by United Artists). Opened 29 October. 125 minutes.

Bath night in Baker Street, from *The Private Life of Sherlock Holmes* (1970). Robert Stephens in the tub as Holmes, Colin Blakely as Watson, Irene Handl as Mrs Hudson.

1972

THE HOUND OF THE BASKERVILLES

American TV movie adaptation
adap: Robert E. Thompson, dir: Barry Crane
Stewart Granger as Sherlock Holmes
Bernard Fox as Doctor Watson
with William Shatner as Stapleton, Anthony Zerbe as Doctor Mortimer, Sally Ann Howes, John Williams, Ian Ireland as Sir Henry Baskerville, Jane Merrow as Beryl Stapleton, Alan Caillou as Inspector Lestrade, Brendan Dillon as Barrymore, Arline Anderson as Mrs Barrymore, Billy Bowles, Chuck Hicks as Selden, Karen Kondan (prod: Stanley Kallis, Richard Irving for Universal). Shown 12 February (USA). 90 minutes with commercial breaks.

1974

SHERLOCK HOLMES

British stage revival
by William Gillette and Arthur Conan Doyle, dir: Frank Dunlop
John Wood as Sherlock Holmes
Tim Pigott-Smith as Doctor Watson
with Philip Locke as Moriarty, Mary Rutherford as Alice Faulkner, Harry Towb, Barbara Leigh-

The poster for the American presentation of the RSC's production of Sherlock Holmes (1974).

Hunt, Nicholas Selby, Trevor Peacock, Martin Milman, Sean Clarke as Billy, Morgan Sheppard. Opened 1 January (Royal Shakespeare Company production at Aldwych Theatre, London).

SHERLOCK HOLMES

American stage revival
by William Gillette and Arthur Conan Doyle, dir: Frank Dunlop
John Wood as Sherlock Holmes
Dennis Cooney as Doctor Watson
with Philip Locke as Moriarty, Lynne Lipton as Alice Faulkner, Richard Lupino, Christina Pickles, Ron Randell, Tony Tanner, Tobias Haller as Billy, Robert Phalen, Richard Woods. Opened 12 November (Royal Shakespeare Company production at Broadhurst Theater, New York).

Patrick Horgan, John Neville and Robert Stephens later replaced John Wood as Sherlock Holmes; Clive Revill and Alan Sues later replaced Philip Locke as Moriarty; Diana Kirkwood later replaced Lynne Lipton as Alice Faulkner.

A STUDY IN SCARLET

British radio adaptation
adap: Michael Hardwick, dir: Roger Pine
Robert Powell as Sherlock Holmes
Dinsdale Landon as Doctor Watson
with Frederick Treves as Inspector Gregson, John Hollis as Inspector Lestrade, Don Fellows as Jefferson Hope. Heard 25 December.

DOCTOR WATSON AND THE DARKWATER HALL MYSTERY

British television production
sc: Kingsley Amis, dir: James Cellan Jones
Edward Fox as Doctor Watson
with Elaine Taylor, Christopher Cazenove, Marguerite Young as Mrs Hudson (prod: Mark Shivas for BBC TV). Shown 27 December. 70 minutes.

1975

THE ADVENTURE OF SHERLOCK HOLMES' SMARTER BROTHER

American film production (shot in England)
sc & dir: Gene Wilder
Douglas Wilmer as Sherlock Holmes
Thorley Walters as Doctor Watson
with Gene Wilder as Sigerson Holmes, Madeline Kahn, Marty Feldman, Dom DeLuise, Leo McKern as Moriarty, Roy Kinnear, John Le Mesurier, George Silver, Susan Field, John Hollis, Albert Finney (prod: Richard A. Roth for Jouer productions, distributed by 20th Century-Fox). Released December. 91 minutes.

1976

SHERLOCK HOLMES IN NEW YORK

American TV movie/film production
sc: Alvin Sapinsley, dir: Boris Sagal
Roger Moore as Sherlock Holmes
Patrick Macnee as Doctor Watson
Marjorie Bennett as Mrs Hudson
with John Huston as Moriarty, Gig Young, Charlotte Rampling as Irene Adler, David Huddleston, Signe Hasso, Leon Ames, John Abbott, Jackie Coogan, Maria Grimm, Geoffrey Moore, Alvin Sapinsley (prod: John Cutts for 20th Century-Fox). Shown 18 October (USA). 2 hours with commercial breaks.

THE SEVEN-PER-CENT SOLUTION

American film production (based in England)
sc: Nicholas Meyer from his novel, dir: Herbert Ross
Nicol Williamson as Sherlock Holmes
Robert Duvall as Doctor Watson
Alison Leggatt as Mrs Hudson
with Alan Arkin as Sigmund Freud, Vanessa Redgrave, Laurence Olivier as Moriarty, Joel Grey, Samantha Eggar as Mary Watson, Jeremy Kemp, Charles Gray as Mycroft Holmes, Georgia Brown, Regine, Anna Quayle, Jill Townsend as Mrs Holmes, John Bird, Leon Greene as Squire Holmes, Michael Blagdon as young Holmes, Sheila Shand Gibbs (prod: Herbert Ross for Universal). Released October. 113 minutes.

Holmes (Nicol Williamson) and Watson (Robert Duvall) in *The Seven-Per-Cent Solution* (1976).

1977

SILVER BLAZE

British television adaptation
adap: Julian Bond, dir: John Davies
Christopher Plummer as Sherlock Holmes
Thorley Walters as Doctor Watson
with Basil Henson as Colonel Ross, Gary Watson as Inspector Gregory, Richard Beale as Straker,

Donald Burton as Fitzroy-Simpson, Barry Lineham as Silas Brown, Josie Kidd as Mrs Straker (prod: William Denteen for Harlech TV). First shown 27 November. 30 minutes.

1978

THE CRUCIFER OF BLOOD
American stage production
by Paul Giovanni, partly from *The Sign of the Four*, dir: Paul Giovanni
Paxton Whitehead as Sherlock Holmes
Timothy Landfield as Doctor Watson
with Glenn Close as Mary Morstan, Christopher Curry as Jonathan Small, Stephen Keep as Major John Sholto, Bill Herndon, Ian Trigger, Tuck Mulligan, Greg Houston, Melvin Lum, T. Ervin as Tonga (prod: Studio Arena Theater, Buffalo, New York). Opened 6 January. Re-opened at Helen Hayes Theater, New York, on 28 September 1978 with Whitehead, Landfield and most of original cast. Opened in London at the Theatre Royal, Haymarket, March 1979 with Keith Michell as Holmes and Denis Lill as Watson under the direction of Paul Giovanni.

British radio adaptations
Barry Foster as Sherlock Holmes
David Buck as Doctor Watson
Thirteen stories produced by BBC Birmingham, each 30 minutes.
The Red-Headed League (adap: Michael Bakewell, dir: Roger Pine). Heard 4 June.
The Musgrave Ritual (adap: Michael Bakewell, dir: Roger Pine). Heard 11 June.
Silver Blaze (adap: Michael Bakewell, dir: Roger Pine). Heard 18 June.
The Naval Treaty (adap: Bill Morrison, dir: Peter Novis). Heard 25 June.
The Priory School (adap: Michael Bakewell, dir: Peter Novis). Heard 2 July.
Charles Augustus Milverton (adap: Bill Morrison, dir: Peter Novis). Heard 9 July.
The Copper Beeches (adap: Michael Bakewell, dir: Vanessa Whitburn). Heard 16 July.
The Blue Carbuncle (adap: Bill Morrison, dir: Peter Novis). Heard 23 July.
The Reigate Squires (adap: Bill Morrison, dir: Peter Novis). Heard 30 July.
The Solitary Cyclist (adap & dir: Michael Bakewell). Heard 6 August.
The Six Napoleons (adap: Bill Morrison, dir: Roger Pine). Heard 13 August.
The Abbey Grange (adap & dir: Michael Bakewell). Heard 20 August.
The Disappearance of Lady Frances Carfax (adap: Michael Bakewell, dir: Roger Pine). Heard 27 August.

1979

MURDER BY DECREE
British-Canadian film production
sc: John Hopkins, from *The Ripper File* by John Lloyd, Elwyn Jones, dir: Bob Clark
Christopher Plummer as Sherlock Holmes
James Mason as Doctor Watson
Betty Woolfe as Mrs Hudson
with David Hemmings, Susan Clark, Anthony Quayle, John Gielgud, Frank Finlay as Inspector Lestrade, Donald Sutherland, Genevieve Bujold, Chris Wiggins, Teddi Moore, Peter Jonfield, Roy Lansford, Catherine Kessler, Ron Pember, June Brown, Iris Fry, Geoffrey Russell, Victor

Langeley, Pamela Abbott, Robin Marchall (prod: Rene Dupont, Bob Clark for Saucy Jack/Decree, distributed in USA by Avco Embassy, in Britain by Warner Bros.). Released January. 112 minutes.

1981

Australian animation adaptations
SHERLOCK HOLMES AND THE BASKERVILLE CURSE
adap from *The Hound of the Baskervilles*
Peter O'Toole as the voice of Sherlock Holmes
with the voices of Helen Morse, Ron Haddrick.
THE SIGN OF FOUR, A STUDY IN SCARLET, A VALLEY OF FEAR (prod: Eddy Graham). Each 52 minutes.

SHERLOCK HOLMES
Televised American stage production
by William Gillette and Arthur Conan Doyle, dir: Gary Halverson, Peter H. Hunt
Frank Langella as Sherlock Holmes
Richard Woods as Doctor Watson
with Laurie Kennedy as Alice Faulkner, George Morfogen as Moriarty, Tom Atkins, Susan Clark, Stephen Collins, William Duell, John Tillinger, Dwight Schultz, Babette Tweed (prod: Peter H. Hunt at the Williamstown Theater Festival, Massachusetts, before a live audience). Shown 15 November onwards on HBO. 150 minutes (tape).

1982

SHERLOCK HOLMES AND DOCTOR WATSON
American television series (made in Poland)
Geoffrey Whitehead as Sherlock Holmes
Donald Pickering as Doctor Watson
Twenty-five episodes produced and mostly written by Sheldon Reynolds, directed by Reynolds and Val Guest, a few based on the Conan Doyle stories (including **The Case of the Speckled Band**). First shown (eleven episodes) on West German television in 1982.

THE HOUND OF THE BASKERVILLES
British television adaptation
adap: Alexander Baron, dir: Peter Duguid
Tom Baker as Sherlock Holmes
Terence Rigby as Doctor Watson
with Will Knightley as Doctor Mortimer, Nicholas Woodeson as Sir Henry Baskerville, Morris Perry

Tom Baker as Holmes in *The Mask of Moriarty* (1985).

as Barrymore, Gillian Martell as Mrs Barrymore, Christopher Ravenscroft as Stapleton, Kay Ashead as Beryl Stapleton, Michael Goldie as Selden, Caroline John as Laura Lyons, Hubert Rees as Inspector Lestrade, John Boswall, Terry Forrestal, Joanna Andrews (prod: Barry Letts for BBC TV). Shown in four 30-minute episodes weekly from 3 October.

YOUNG SHERLOCK
British television production
sc: Gerald Frow, dir: Nicholas Ferguson
Guy Henry as Sherlock Holmes
with June Barry, Christopher Villiers, John Fraser, Heather Chasen, Eva Griffith, Jane Lowe, David Ryde-Futcher, Tim Brierley, Zuleika Robson, Marina McConnell (prod: Pieter Rogers for Granada TV). Shown in eight episodes (1 hour, then 30 minutes, including commercial breaks) from 31 October to 19 December.

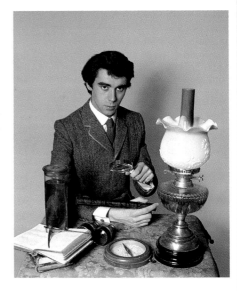

Guy Henry as *Young Sherlock* (1982).

1983

THE SIGN OF FOUR
American TV movie adaptation (shot in England)
adap: Charles Pogue, dir: Desmond Davis
Ian Richardson as Sherlock Holmes
David Healy as Doctor Watson
with Thorley Walters as Major John Sholto, Joe Melia as Jonathan Small, Cherie Lunghi as Mary Morstan, Michael O'Hagan as Mordecai Smith, Terence Rigby, John Pedrick (prod: Otto Plaschkes for Mapleton Films). Shown 13 May (Cannes Film Festival, market section).

THE HOUND OF THE BASKERVILLES
American TV movie adaptation (shot in England)
adap: Charles Pogue, dir: Douglas Hickox
Ian Richardson as Sherlock Holmes
Donald Churchill as Doctor Watson
with Martin Shaw as Sir Henry Baskerville, Nicholas Clay as Stapleton, Denholm Elliott as Doctor Mortimer, Ronald Lacey as Inspector Lestrade, Glynis Barber as Beryl Stapleton, Edward Judd as Barrymore, Eleanor Bron as Mrs Barrymore, Brian Blessed (prod: Otto Plaschkes for Mapleton Films). Shown 15 May (Cannes Film Festival, non-competing).

1984

THE ADVENTURES OF SHERLOCK HOLMES
British television adaptations
Jeremy Brett as Sherlock Holmes
David Burke as Doctor Watson
Rosalie Williams as Mrs Hudson
Seven stories developed by John Hawkesworth and produced by Michael Cox for Granada TV, each one hour (with commercial breaks).
A Scandal in Bohemia (adap: Alexander Baron, dir: Paul Annett) with Gayle Hunnicutt as Irene Adler, Wolf Kähler as King of Bohemia. Shown 24 April.
The Dancing Men (adap: Anthony Skene, dir: John Bruce) with Tenniel Evans as Hilton Cubitt, Eugene Lipinski as Abe Slaney, Betsy Brantley as Elsie Cubitt. Shown 1 May.
The Naval Treaty (adap: Jeremy Paul, dir: Alan Grint) with David Gwillim as Percy Phelps, Gareth Thomas as Joseph Harrison, Alison Skilbeck as Annie Harrison, Ronald Russell as Lord Holdhurst. Shown 8 May.
The Solitary Cyclist (adap: Alan Plater, dir: Paul Annett) with Barbara Wilshere as Violet Smith, John Castle as Carruthers, Michael Siberry as Woodley, Ellis Dale as Williamson. Shown 15 May.
The Crooked Man (adap: Alfred Shaughnessy, dir: Alan Grint) with Norman Jones as Henry Wood, Lisa Daniely as Nancy Barclay, Denys Hawthorne as Colonel James Barclay, Fiona Shaw as Miss Morrison. Shown 22 May.
The Speckled Band (adap: Jeremy Paul, dir: John Bruce) with Jeremy Kemp as Doctor Grimesby Roylott, Rosalyn Landor as Helen Stoner, Denise Armon as Julia Stoner. Shown 29 May.
The Blue Carbuncle (adap: Paul Finney, dir: David Carson) with Frank Middlemass as Henry Baker, Ken Campbell as James Ryder, Frank Mills as Peterson. Shown 5 June.

THE MASKS OF DEATH
British TV film
sc: N. J. Crisp from a story by John Elder, dir: Roy Ward Baker
Peter Cushing as Sherlock Holmes
John Mills as Doctor Watson
Jenny Laird as Mrs Hudson
with Anne Baxter as Irene Adler, Ray Milland, Anton Diffring, Gordon Jackson as Inspector Alec MacDonald, Susan Penhaligon, Marcus Gilbert (prod: Kevin Francis, Norman Priggen for Tyburn). Shown 23 December (Channel 4). 90 minutes with commercial breaks.

1985

THE ADVENTURES OF SHERLOCK HOLMES (second series)
British television adaptations
Jeremy Brett as Sherlock Holmes
David Burke as Doctor Watson
Rosalie Williams as Mrs Hudson
Six stories developed by John Hawkesworth and produced by Michael Cox for Granada TV, each one hour (with commercial breaks).
The Copper Beeches (adap: Bill Craig, dir: Paul Annett) with Joss Ackland as Jephro Rucastle, Natasha Richardson as Violet Hunter. Shown 25 August.

The Greek Interpreter (adap: Derek Marlowe, dir: Alan Grint) with Charles Gray as Mycroft Holmes, Alkis Kritikos as Mr Melas, George Costigan as Wilson Kemp, Nick Field as Harold Latimer, Anton Alexander as Paul Kratides, Oliver Maguire as Inspector Gregson. Shown 1 September.
The Norwood Builder (adap: Richard Harris, dir: Ken Grieve) with Rosalie Crutchley as Mrs Lexington, Colin Jeavons as Inspector Lestrade, Matthew Solon as John Hector McFarlane, Jonathan Adams as Jonas Oldacre. Shown 8 September.
The Resident Patient (adap: Derek Marlowe, dir: David Carson) with Nicholas Clay as Doctor Percy Trevelyan, Patrick Newell as Blessington. Shown 15 September.
The Red-Headed League (adap: John Hawkesworth, dir: John Bruce) with Roger Harwood as Jabez Wilson, Richard Wilson as Duncan Ross, Tim McInnerny as Vincent Spaulding. Shown 22 September.
The Final Problem (adap: John Hawkesworth, dir: Alan Grint) with Eric Porter as Moriarty. Shown 29 September.

THE MASK OF MORIARTY
Irish stage production
by Hugh Leonard, dir: Brian de Salvo
Tom Baker as Sherlock Holmes
Alan Stanford as Doctor Watson
with Ingrid Craigie, Peter Dix as Inspector Lestrade, Brian Munn as Moriarty, Aiden Grennell, David Henry, Cinzia Hardy, William Boyde, Christopher Casson, Daniel Reardon. Opened 4 October (Gate Theatre, Dublin).

YOUNG SHERLOCK HOLMES
American film production (shot in England)
sc: Chris Columbus, dir: Barry Levinson
Nicholas Rowe as Sherlock Holmes
Alan Cox as John Watson
Roger Ashton-Griffiths as Lestrade

with Sophie Ward, Anthony Higgins, Susan Fleetwood, Freddie Jones, Nigel Stock, Earl Rhodes, Brian Oulton, Patrick Newell, Donald Eccles (prod: Mark Johnson for Amblin Entertainment, distributed by Paramount). Opened December. 109 minutes. (Retitled *Sherlock Holmes and the Pyramid of Fear* in England for publicity purposes.)

1986

THE RETURN OF SHERLOCK HOLMES
British television adaptations
Jeremy Brett as Sherlock Holmes
Edward Hardwicke as Doctor Watson
Rosalie Williams as Mrs Hudson
Stories developed by John Hawkesworth and produced by June Wyndham Davies (executive producer: Michael Cox) for Granada TV, each one hour long (with commercial breaks).
The Abbey Grange (adap: Trevor Bowen, dir: Peter Hammond) with Paul Williamson as Inspector Hopkins, Conrad Phillips as Sir Eustace Brackenstall, Anne Louise Lambert as Lady Mary Brackenstall, Zulema Dene as Theresa Wright, Oliver Tobias as Captain Crocker.
The Musgrave Ritual (adap: Jeremy Paul, dir: David Carson) with Michael Culver as Reginald Musgrave, James Hazeldine as Brunton, Johanna Kirby as Rachel Howells.
The Second Stain (adap: John Hawkesworth, dir: John Bruce) with Stuart Wilson as the Rt Hon Trelawney Hope, Patricia Hodge as Lady Hilda, Harry Andrews as Lord Bellinger, Colin Jeavons as Inspector Lestrade, Sean Scanlan as P. C. MacPherson.
The Empty House (adap: John Hawkesworth) with Patrick Allen as Colonel Sebastian Moran, Colin Jeavons as Inspector Lestrade, Paul Lacoux as the Hon. Ronald Adair.

Alan Cox as young Watson and Nicholas Rowe as the young detective in *Young Sherlock Holmes*.

INDEX

ACKNOWLEDGEMENTS

Specific illustrations are courtesy of/copyright of the following:

Abbey National Building Society   127 (centre, centre right)
Amblin Entertainment   124, 141
BBC Publications   106 (top two), 110, 138 (bottom)
British Library   43, 44, 46 (top), 47, 48, 55 (top), 73, 74 (top)
City of Westminster Libraries; Sherlock Holmes Collection, Marylebone Library   2–3, 12, 19, 20, 99, 127, 130
Columbia-EMI-Warner/Avco Embassy   120
Compton/Tekli/Sir Nigel   108 (top, bottom), 138
Gate Theatre, Dublin   121, 140 (bottom)
Granada Television   9 (right), 124 (left), 125, 140 (right)
Hammer/United Artists   105 (top, centre), 136
London Regional Transport   7, 74 (bottom)
Museum of Modern Art   58
National Film Archive   52, 57, 62, 63, 64, 67 (right), 68, 69, 80, 82, 83, 84, 85, 86, 87, 90, 93, 94, 96, 105 (top, centre), 108, 111, 112, 113, 114, 115 (left), 118, 131, 132, 133, 134, 135 (top), 136 (left), 139 (left, right)
National Portrait Gallery   76, 78 (bottom)
Newman-Foreman/Universal   115 (left)
New York Public Library at Lincoln Centre, Performing Arts Research Centre   35, 103
Phalanx/Mirisch/Sir Nigel   111, 112, 113, 114, 139 (left)
Royal Shakespeare Company/The Shakespeare Centre   117, 139 (top centre)
The Stanley MacKenzie Collection   10 (centre, right), 13 (right), 14 (left), 17, 18, 19 (lower right), 21, 36, 37, 38, 39, 41, 42 (left), 45, 50, 53 (top), 54, 56, 57 (top two), 66, 70, 71, 72, 99 (left), 104, 107 (left), 109, 123 (right), 126, 136 (right)
Syndication International   53 (left), 54 (right), 79
20th Century-Fox   122, 123 (top)
Universal   118, 139 (right)

Unlike Inspector G. Lestrade, who happily took credit for the patient sleuthing of S. Holmes, I am more than anxious to acknowledge the massive body of scholarship from which this overview of the Sherlock Holmes phenomenon has benefited. It would take half a lifetime to read closely all the material that has been gathered in the Sherlock Holmes Collection at the Marylebone Library, Marylebone Road, London NW1, where items are publicly available on demand (consult the newly published catalogue of its riches, *The Contents of a Lumber-Room*, price £5 plus postage). I thank the Collection's librarian, Catherine Cooke, for her hospitable assistance, as well as Richard Bowden and the other staff who always made me welcome in her absence. The British Film Institute and the British Library were of considerable supplementary assistance.

Thanks to the magnificent co-operation of Stanley MacKenzie, I am able to illustrate some of the gems of his private collection, many of them never before reproduced in colour as book illustrations. Stanley could not have been more helpful, and it is a great pleasure to record this book's indebtedness to the Stanley MacKenzie Collection.

My friends Pat Billings, Barrie Fishman, Bernard Hrusa-Marlow, Alvin H. Marill and Tom Vallance were as dependably helpful as on previous occasions, and I greatly appreciate their support, while other friends, Barbara and John Cutts, responded beyond all expectations in searching their lumber-room for useful material. Vernica Hitchcock's catholic interests are regularly assisting my literary undertakings – thanks again, Veronica.

My wife Lesley provided some intrepid chauffeuring into the wilds of Southsea, South Norwood and the New Forest for on-the-spot research, while Lesley Doick did a fine job in assisting with the preparation of the final manuscript. Mary Flower researched American sources with her customary diligence.

Among others (although I hope there are no omissions), I have been encouraged by the generous help of Nikki Caparan of the Abbey National Building Society; Peter Durrant of London Regional Transport; John Edwards; Miss M. Godfrey and John Thorn of Portsmouth Central Library (Hampshire Library Service); Joan and Eddie Hardcastle at the Sherlock Holmes Public House and Restaurant; J. W. Miller at St Bartholomew's Hospital; Jackie Morris, Tise Vahimagi and others at the National Film Archive (Viewing Service and Stills Library); Andrew Robinson and Joan Riley of Granada Television; Marie Rooney of the Gate Theatre, Dublin; Don Smith of *Radio Times*; and Daphne Walsh of Preview One.

Let me urge my keener British readers, if they haven't done so already, to join the Sherlock Holmes Society of London (see footnote on page 101 for address), not just for the stimulation of its learned magazine, *The Sherlock Holmes Journal*, but for the friendly atmosphere of its lectures, film shows and trips. The game is still afoot, as played by such prominent members as Patsy Dalton, Bernard Davies, Roger Johnson, Heather and Tim Owen, Geoffrey Stavert and Jeffrey Thrift, and long will it continue.

This book is for the McChesneys – Doris, Cecil, Bill, and in memory of Gordon – for their well-remembered hospitality, and for other friends of my Delaware days.